A SUBMARINE AT WAR

THE

BRIEF LIFE

of

HMS *TROOPER*

Battle Honours

Mediterranean   1943

Sicily   1943

Aegean   1943

Launched 5th March 1942 – Lost c. 17th October 1943

by

David Renwick Grant

Foreword by
Captain Richard Wraith CBE Royal Navy

First published in 2006 by

Periscope Publishing Ltd

33 Barwis Terrace

Penzance

Cornwall TR18 2AW

Copyright © David Renwick Grant

All rights reserved. No part of this book may be reproduced or transmitted in any form or by any means, electronic or mechanical, including photocopying, recording, or by any information storage and retrieval system, without permission in writing from the publisher.

A CIP record for this book is available from the British Library

ISBN No 1-904381-33-2

Printed and bound by Antony Rowe Ltd, Eastbourne

List of illustrations

At Port Said 1943	53
In the Clyde	53
Crest	54
Seamen's Mess	55
Lt J S Wraith DSO DSC RN	56
Ldg Seaman L Williams	57
L/Tel. Len Thompson	58
HMS *Thunderbolt* alongside Depot Ship HMS *Titania*	59
Lt Guy Clarabut DSO RN	59
Italian Submarine *Pietro Micca*	60
Officers on Bridge	60
Lt LAS Grant DSC RN	61
ERA Allison Gillies	61
Seven "Troopers"	62
Trooper on Trial	62
Chariot in Loch Cairnbawn	63
Trooper with Chariots	63
The Jolly Roger	64
ERA Forbes	64

List of Contents

	Page
Foreword	6
Author's Preface	8
Statistics & Time Line	10
Introductory	12
Trooper's Story	17
Members of the crew – last patrol	114
Acknowledgements	115
Bibliography	116
Index	122

Dedicated to the crew

of

His Majesty's Submarine

Trooper

&

to all those who served in submarines

and in so many cases gave their lives

for our freedom

and especially to

Lt L A S Grant DSC RN

Foreword

In January 2004 David Grant wrote to me explaining that he was researching the history of HMS *Trooper* in which his half-brother, Lieutenant Alick Grant, and my father, Lieutenant Johnnie Wraith, had both served, as First Lieutenant and Commanding Officer respectively, when the submarine was lost with all hands in October 1943 in the Aegean. A sadness we both shared in common was that David had never met his brother nor I my father. During our own careers our experience of life could not have been more different. I joined the Royal Navy in 1961 and spent almost all the next 37 years in the submarine service, appointed to 13 submarines and commanding four. David followed a far more learned life as author, ecologist, traveller and Bahá'í, before deciding two years ago to write the story of *Trooper*.

He has managed, in this short book, to bring to life, in a delightful style, the intriguing and exciting tale, spanning some 14 months, in the life of just one of the many Royal Navy submarines that played such a crucial and significant role in the war at sea during World War II. He has almost totally avoided the political nuances and technical detail, to concentrate on the human facets of the war in the Mediterranean.

Life in submarines, before the advent of the colossal nuclear powered boats, was extremely arduous – tiring, smelly, unhealthy, uncomfortable and frequently frightening. Much of this I was personally able to associate with but had always taken for granted; now David Grant has managed to paint this picture of a submariner's life during war in an utterly convincing and easily readable style.

Sadly I was of little help to David in his research as my mother, having been widowed in 1939 when her first husband was lost in HMS *Royal Oak,* was then only married to my father for such a short time before he was killed, that photos and mementoes were scarce and memories very guarded. This book has allowed me to appreciate, more fully, the statement made by Sir Winston Churchill: 'Of all the branches of men in the Forces there is none that shows more devotion and faces greater perils than the submariner. Great deeds are done in the air and on the land; nevertheless nothing surpasses your exploits.'

This book is a delightful cameo of a very small – but highly significant – participant in the war at sea and I feel extremely privileged to have been invited to write the foreword.

Richard Wraith

Author's Preface

I am very conscious of the fact that in writing this account of HMS *Trooper*, almost all of the material in it has been derived from other sources. My own contribution has been confined to that of researcher and narrator. Throughout the writing of it, I have been aware that not only am I not a submariner but also very ignorant of the language of submarines and the sea – even though, after reading many wartime accounts, I sometimes felt that I could romp through the commanding officer's course and take a boat to sea with no bother at all!

On the basis that at least some of the people I hope will be reading this will be as clueless as I was about some of the terms and abbreviations used, I have defined them thus – e.g. 'co. & sp.' [course & speed], or sometimes, especially in the case of ranks, the other way about: Engine Room Artificer [ERA] – on first appearance in the text. A few were not so treated: Asdic, an early form of sonar or echo-location, is actually the acronym for Allied Submarine Detection Investigation Committee. Allusions in a boat's log to 'standing charge' and 'running charge' refer to battery charging. This was done with the submarine on the surface, stopped or while travelling. Quite often, one engine would be used to propel the boat and charge batteries while power from the other was used solely for charging. The term 'watch diving' means that, when a boat was dived but circumstances permitted, some of the watch on duty were allowed to rest. War conditions were stressful, so every opportunity was taken to rest men when possible. Then there is the Jolly Roger. It might well be asked what ships of the Royal Navy were doing flying a pirate flag! In 1901 Admiral Sir Arthur Wilson VC, the Controller of the Royal Navy, said: "*Submarines are underhand, unfair and damned un-English. The crews of all submarines captured should be treated as pirates and hanged*". In response, Lt Cdr (later Admiral Sir) Max Horton flew a Jolly Roger on return to port after sinking the German cruiser SMS *Hela* and the destroyer SMS *S-116* in 1914. In World War II it became customary for submarines to fly their Jolly Rogers on return from successful patrols. Finally, I have been unable to track down information about the nature and extent of sea areas, such as QBB.255. Undoubtedly, however, they were used as part of the system of operational control by Captains (S) – it would have been nice to have details, though.

TROOPER'S STATISTICS AND TIME LINE

Length:	263 ft
Displacement surfaced:	1327 tons
Max. speed surfaced:	15¼ kt
Breadth:	26½ ft
Displacement submerged:	1527 tons
Max. speed submerged:	9 kt
Draught:	14ft 8in

Main Engines

2 Admiralty design 4-stroke single-acting 6 cylinder, 17½ in bore, 18 in stroke, developing 1250 bhp at 480 rpm.

Motors: 2 electric propulsion, each 225 shp.

Batteries: 3, totalling 336 cells.

1939	09 Oct	Ordered
1940	26 May	Keel laid
	May 1941	Bomb damaged [completion delayed 6 months in consequence]
1942	05 Mar	Launched
	29 Aug	Delivered to and accepted by Royal Navy
	29 Aug-04 Nov	Working up in the **Clyde** [Chariot containers fitted during this time]
	05 - 07 Nov	Passage from **Dunoon** to **HHZ** (Loch Cairnbawn)
	08 - 11 Nov	at **HHZ**
	12 Nov	Sailed at Noon for Malta, in company with *P311* and escort *La Capricieuse*
	02 Dec	Arrived **Malta** in afternoon
	03 - 28 Dec	At **Malta**, training with Chariots

29 Dec	Left Malta on *Operation 'Principal'* with *Thunderbolt* and *P311*

1943

	Night of 2nd/3rd Jan 1943, launched 3 Chariots offshore from Palermo; *Thunderbolt launched two* [*P311* lost, presumed mined, near her target, La Maddalena]
07 Jan	Arrived back at **Malta**
08 Jan – 02 Feb	At **Malta** [Chariot containers removed in dockyard]
03 Feb–18 Feb	Left on *2nd War Patrol* [Lt R P Webb temporary CO] Corfu – Levkas – Cephalonia
18 Feb – 04 Mar	At **Malta**
04 Mar	Sailed **Malta** 1300hrs on *3rd War Patrol* N of Messina – Naples approaches – Cap Milazzo [13 Mar – *Thunderbolt* lost]
22 Mar	Arrived **Algiers**
23 Mar–05 Apr	At **Algiers**
05–25 Apr	Sailed on *4th War Patrol* Tyrrhenian Sea – Ustica [blank patrol]
25 Apr–11 May	At **Algiers**
11-17 May	On passage, **Algiers - Malta**
17–22 May	At **Malta**
22 May	Sailed **Malta** on *5th War Patrol* Adriatic + W coast Greece **Ops 'Entertain'** and **'Tiger'** (landing commando groups)
13 Jun	Arrived **Beirut** [propeller damaged by wreckage]
13–26 Jun	At **Beirut**
26–28 Jun	On passage to **Port Said** [Lt G S C Clarabut temporary CO]
28 Jun–07 Jul	At **Port Said** dry dock for new propeller
07 Jul	Sailed Port Said on *6th War Patrol* Adriatic and W coast Greece ***29 Jul sank It. Reg. Submarine *Pietro Micca*
02 Aug	Arrived **Beirut**
02 Aug–20 Aug	At **Beirut**
20 Aug	Sailed on *7th War Patrol* Aegean – Piraeus – Rhodes – Gulf of Salonika – Skiathos
10 Sep	Arrived **Beirut**
10–26 Sep	At **Beirut**
26 Sep	Sailed on *8th War Patrol* W of Dodecanese and Leros
14 Oct	Challenged LSF F8 in **Alinda Bay** [see Seligman: *War in the Islands*]
17 Oct	Not replying to signals; reported overdue.

Introductory

A short description of life aboard wartime submarines

Life on a British World War II submarine was cramped, dirty, smelly, noisy, uncomfortable, difficult and often dangerous. Yet those who were submariners almost never wanted to return to General Service. The six shillings a day extra pay can hardly have made up for being on patrol, usually for about three weeks, during which it was impossible to wash; when after the first few days the food became steadily more inedible; where space was so limited that 'hot bunking' – two men on different watches using the same bed – was normal; where the air became more and more foul the longer the boat was submerged and where being depth-charged after making an attack was the norm.

Fresh food did not last for very long in the warm, foetid atmosphere of a submarine, so after the first few days, steaks and fruit gave way to bully beef and tinned peaches. Stories abound about how the bread, which might well be being slept on by someone before it was all eaten because it took up a lot of space, would go mouldy and become hard. Mould would be cut off and hard loaves would be damped and reconstituted in the boat's oven. Variety dwindled daily. If the patrol was overly extended, quantities of some items might start being rationed. A lot depended on the ability and imagination of the cook.

Fresh water supplies could become even more critical. Only so much could be carried and there was never enough to permit proper washing. During a period dived, air pressure would invariably increase due to leakage from the bottled air. There was a compressor to recompress it and so keep down the pressure, a process that produced quite a lot of water. Although rather smelly and unsuitable for drinking, this water had a soft texture and was excellent for washing. However, its use was eventually officially banned because it contained so many germs, although this prohibition was frequently ignored.

Smokers had a hard time, because smoking was forbidden whilst submerged and this usually meant for periods of many hours. The daily rum ration, however, was served as usual. Under Admiralty regulations, it was supposed to be drunk immediately but many men managed to bottle their tots and save them for a special occasion or for their time ashore at the end of a patrol and a blind eye was usually turned to this practice.

The heads [lavatory] was a fiercesome machine that, if not flushed correctly, resulted in a pressurised blow-back of the contents. Flushing was strictly prohibited near enemy waters, as the resultant discharge might float to the surface, be seen and give away the boat's presence. The same applied to dumping gash [waste]. Thus an accumulation of assorted smells and bacteria often built up and it is perhaps remarkable that submariners remained as healthy as they did.

Ailments were the province of the Coxswain and the Captain. These were mainly confined to boils, skin rashes and minor cuts, which was just as well as there was little provision for dealing with serious injuries in the none-too-clean atmosphere that prevailed aboard. Constipation was a problem for many and occasionally there were outbreaks of diarrhoea.

Lighting was very bright except when dimmed to red during an attack or prior to surfacing. Some ex-submariners have suggested that this may have caused some damage to their sight. As to hearing, engine noise almost certainly did cause a degree of deafness among some crew-members whose stations were in the engine-compartment. The noise from depth-charge explosions was very loud, if close, and when firing, the gun was extremely loud also.

The ultimate danger was of course being sunk. So often this meant a total loss with all hands. However, submariners always maintain that they much preferred that risk to the danger that faced soldiers in a trench, or even that faced by General Service men under shellfire or aircraft attack, where the possibility of being dreadfully wounded was ever-present. Several boats were brought to the surface by depth-charging. Most of their crews were rescued and taken prisoner but with one exception

– the incredibly gallant *Seal* – their crews managed to scuttle them before the enemy could capture and secure them.

I have given this outline of what conditions aboard a submarine were like, because I felt it was necessary for a clearer understanding of what follows. However I have not tried to interpolate the experiences of others, on other boats, into this account, and have used only what is available for His Majesty's Submarine *Trooper*. There exist some excellent descriptions of life in boats written by submariners, both by commanding officers and crewmen, which describe patrols and actions in detail. Their titles are given in the bibliography and I refer anyone interested to one, or several, of these.

It has not been easy to piece together this account of *Trooper*. Her active life, from her commissioning in August 1942 to her loss in October 1943 was a brief but action-packed fourteen months. Of those who served on her, the majority shared her fate. The personal information available came mainly from a diary kept by one of her Engine-room Artificers, Peter Forbes, and the journal of one of her officers, Sub-Lieutenant Neil Campbell, with additions from the few other surviving men who were not on that fateful final patrol. Everything else has been uncovered in official files at The National Archives (Public Record Office), Royal Navy Submarine Museum, Imperial War Museum, a number of books and from the extensive records of Scotts Shipbuilding & Engineering Co Ltd, of Greenock.

The T-class submarines were Britain's largest and newest design. They still lacked something in speed, both on the surface and dived, but had the formidable capacity of being able to fire a 10-torpedo bow salvo. The first to be launched, of a total of 53 built, was *Triton*, in October 1937. The pressure hull, within which was contained most of the equipment and the crew's accommodation, was only 16½ feet in diameter at its maximum. The main cylinder of this pressure hull was divided into six compartments by bulkheads, each with a watertight door. From bow to stern, these compartments were: the torpedo tube space; the torpedo reload compartment (better known as the fore-ends); main crew accommodation including officers and wardroom; control room and captain's cabin; engine room and after-ends. Beneath all of these except the engine-room were spaces that housed batteries, fuel, and fresh water. Most of the equipment required for operating the boat, including periscopes and Asdic, was located in the control room. Space also had to be found for the galley and all the stores. It was always at a premium and much of it was filled with a complicated maze of machinery.

The crew of a T-class submarine was normally about 60 strong. The captain would be a Lieutenant or sometimes a Lieutenant Commander, who had taken and passed the Submarine Commander's Course, known universally as 'The Perisher.' His First Lieutenant, the boat's executive officer, colloquially called the Jimmy, would also be a Lieutenant, as would the 'third hand.' The other officers (usually three) and the ratings were all specialists of one sort or another but duties often overlapped. For example, the torpedo attack team would have the Electrical Artificer [EA] and the Signalman in it, while the Cook and the Wardroom Steward were members of the gun's crew. Apart from the Coxswain, the Chief Engine Room Artificer [CERA] and probably the Captain, everyone would be in their early or mid-twenties or even late teens.

A curious and unique smell pervaded the boats. It consisted of a whiff of diesel overlying the rather cloying odour of oil and grease, on top of which would be a tinge of background battery smell, a tang of salt from the inevitable accumulation of drips and seeps and a dash of lanolin from oiled wool clothing. At times there would be food smells, sometimes the reek of vomit and disinfectant and always a gradual build-up of human sweat, for submariners, with no proper opportunity for washing, unavoidably soon became pretty grubby.

After being submerged for the day and especially when kept down for prolonged periods by the enemy, the air would become very foul, soporific and warm, lacking the proper proportion of oxygen to carbon dioxide. At its most serious, CO_2 [carbon dioxide] poisoning begins, which impairs judgement. Physically walking a few paces brings on temporary exhaustion and having to apply force to an object produces "a burning at the pit of the lungs so consuming that one's diaphragm and abdomen seem in danger of falling apart."

Even a good imagination and extensive reading of first-hand accounts cannot begin to do justice to the reality of life on board a wartime submarine. Only those who have served on boats really know what it was really like. Inadequate though it nevertheless is, however, this description should be borne in mind as the backdrop common to all submarines when reading the story of just one of them, HMS *Trooper* herself.

TROOPER'S STORY

The morning of Saturday 29th August 1942 on the Clyde was fine. The barometer was high, the wind south-east force three and the visibility good. At Scotts Shipbuilding & Engineering Co Ltd, the clang of hammers and the heavy thud of rivets being driven home continued apace. Now and then a shout would ring out above the din. The bustle of this wartime work was replicated around all the Clyde yards, as Britain desperately built new ships to replace her mounting losses. The war was at a critical stage and victory was not yet in sight.

Down at Scotts' basin lay a brand-new submarine, her paint still pristine, with a small knot of sailors and yard workers busy about her. It was just 11 am. Up in the company offices, a naval lieutenant knocked on a door marked *J N Hutchison, Shipyard Director* and entered. The self-same Mr Hutchison rose from behind his desk and shook hands with his visitor before turning to pick up a form from his desk. It stated "We, Messrs. Scotts Shipbuilding and Engineering Company Limited, Greenock, at/off Greenock handed over this 29th of August, one thousand nine hundred and forty two, at 1100 o'clock, J.1108 constructed by us for His Majesty's Navy." Under this was stamped the company name with Mr Hutchison's signature newly added.

The officer read the brief paragraph and then the one below, which said "Received from Messrs. Scotts Shipbuilding and Engineering Company Limited, Greenock, J.1108 this 29th day of August, One thousand nine hundred and forty two without prejudice to outstanding liabilities." Then came a blank space above the words 'Commanding Officer.' The lieutenant took out a pen and neatly signed 'J. S. Wraith' in the space. J.1108, a submarine that had cost £349,364 to build and incidentally netted Scotts a useful £114,913 profit, was now officially his responsibility. He said goodbye to Hutchison, left his office and made his way down to the basin.

As he came to the boat, he paused briefly to look at the name embossed on her conning tower: *Trooper*. Job number J.1108 had just become the latest addition to the Royal Navy's growing stock of T-class submarines. Wraith wondered momentarily what the future held for her, then strode purposefully along to the gangway and boarded his new command.

* * *

Trooper had almost never even reached the water. She had been ordered in October 1939 and her keel was laid on the 26th March 1940. On the night of 6th-7th May 1941, she was sitting on her building blocks, alongside her sister ship HMS/m *Traveller*, when Greenock suffered one of the many heavy air raids inflicted upon it during the war. Some of the tons of bombs raining down fell on Scotts' yard, which was hard hit by this attack, and Job No. 1108 was slewed off her blocks, canted longitudinally and transversely and suffered damage to her stern. Job No. 1107 – *Traveller* – was more fortunate, suffering only a slight shift of her stern. The bomb damage to *Trooper* caused considerable delay in her completion, for though *Traveller* was launched on 27th August 1941, it would be more than six months after that before her sister took to the river.

The launch of J.1108 was a low-key affair. The invitation to perform the naming ceremony that was sent to Mrs Mathias, wife of the Warship Production Superintendent for the Scottish Area, specifically stated "As it is war-time, there will be no public ceremony." Her acceptance noted that only her husband would accompany her "as I know how important it is to limit the number of guests." Thus on Thursday 5th March 1942, at 2.40 p.m., at a quiet little gathering, similar to many that took place in those terrible years, Mrs Mathias cracked a bottle over the bows of the undignified 'J.1108' and turned her into proud, sleek HMS/m *Trooper*. The small ceremonial party that had gathered for the launch, together with the men who had built her, watched as she slid smoothly into the Clyde's turbid waters.

One of those men was probably John S Taylor, a plater in the yard but also an accomplished artist who had exhibited at the Royal Scottish Academy, the Royal Scottish Society of Painters in Watercolours and the Royal Glasgow Institute of Fine Arts between the wars. His work was mostly devoted to marine subjects and he painted many of the ships he helped to construct, including the submarines *Tribune, Spark, Strongbow* and *Artful*, as well as a picture of *Trooper*.

Almost four months of further work had to follow before *Trooper* was ready to hand over to the Navy. This was her 'Programme of Trials, Tests and Inspections'. The list of things to be checked was long. It began with the high-pressure air system, included such items as rigging the wireless transmission [W/T] aerials, preliminary hydrophone and echo sounding trials, trials of torpedo and mining equipment, checks of the gyro compass and a 'basin trim' where the main tanks were flooded and blown. Also in Scotts' basin, the diesel engines and electric motors were run up and a lot more done besides, before Preliminary Sea Trials were scheduled, "to be carried out inside Boom between Cloch Point and Loch Long." Then came "Diving Trials (In Gareloch) ," followed by gun trials and "8 hours Full power trials." Finally, after the gun was test-fired, after everything that needed to be calibrated had been calibrated, after all the electrical systems and the torpedo equipment had been tested and a last motor and engine run made, the boat was ready to leave its makers and join His Majesty's Navy. It was 29th August, 1942.

Since January, one or two of the crew had been present, 'standing by' as it is known. Their job was to shadow the shipyard's men, make suggestions for minor alterations and improvements and to familiarise themselves with everything they needed to know about their vessel. One of them was ERA Allison Gillies. "There were two or possibly three of us. Myself and someone from the upper deck," he told me. "A few more came after the launch, including electricians. My job was to watch all the machinery as it was going into the ship to make sure everything was ok. Sometimes they [dockyard workers] tried to cut corners, y'know. I had to check everything, even the engine alignment. The whole crew only came in June, after dock trials." These included Lt L A S Grant, my half-brother. "He was all right."

* * *

As soon as Wraith stepped aboard, he began preparing *Trooper* to sail, though she was only moving a short distance as her log shows:

H. M. Submarine *Trooper* Saturday 29th Day of August 1942 From Greenock to Holy Loch and at Holy Loch

1130	Final inspection completed; ship accepted from Messrs Scotts S. & E. Co., Ltd. of Greenock. Hands employed embarking kit etc.
1330	Harbour Stations
1400	1405 Slipped from Scotts' basin & proceeded co. & sp. as req. for leaving Clyde Channel (Main Motors).
1415	Off "tail o' the Bank." Changed to Main Engines, co & sp [course & speed] as req. for proceeding to Holy Loch.
1450	Main Engines [ME] Lubrication System failed. Changed to Main Motors [MM]. Fall out Harbour Station: special sea dutymen.
1450	Harbour Stations.
1515	Secured star. Side to on H.M.S. Forth outboard of P213. [HMS/m *Saracen*][1]
1600	S.P.s [Secret/Special Publications]. mustered and correct. [initialled] LASG.

Thus ended the first day of what was to be a very intensive two months on the Clyde for *Trooper*, working up to operational readiness. The following extracts from her log give a glimpse of what that time was like. One must fill in, in one's imagination, the roar of the engines, the muttering and cursing that accompanied the loading of torpedoes, the expletives that must have followed the accidental discharge of a torpedo on 11th September and the fun that was had on the gunnery exercise on 24th, which included a night shoot. The more important activities have been underlined and names of ships and other submarines capitalised.

31.08.42 Holy Loch to Inchmarnock Water and at Holy Loch. 1300 One rating dangerously ill. 1850 SPO discharged ill to FORTH. [Depot ship]

01.09.42 Holy Loch to Kilbrennan Sound.

01.09.42 1708 Exercised "Captain(S)" gun action.

---

[1] Originally P63, renumbered P213. Renumbered P247 to remove the unlucky '13'. Sank German s/m *U335*, while on work-up in North Sea between Shetlands and Norway, 3rd Aug 42, and then Italian s/m *Granito* off northwest Sicily, 9th Nov 1942. 7th Aug 42 forced to the surface, off Bastia, NE coast of Corsica in Tyrrhenian Sea - by depth charges from Italian corvettes *Minerva* and *Euterpe*. Crew abandoned ship but scuttled the boat.

03.09.42 Kilbrennan Sound to Holy Loch. Alongside FORTH.

04.09.42 Holy Loch. Embarking torpedoes.

2200   'Immediate Readiness' (weather).

0800   Secured to No.6 buoy. 1000 film party aboard for official duty.

1635   back to FORTH.

07.09.42 Holy Loch to Loch Long. 1840   Anchored in 11 fathoms.

08.09.42 Loch Long. <u>Torpedo trials on range</u>.

1110 Fired No.1;

1212   No.2;

1303   No.3;

1343   No.4:

1428   No.5;

1507   No.6;

1730   GRAPH[2] secured alongside.

09.09.42 (Arrochar)

Of course, short spells of leave were given even during this busy time. Agnes Gillies, or Nessie as she prefers to be called, recalls travelling to Arrochar on the train to visit Allison for the weekend. They had not been long married at that time. When she got off the train, the wife of one of *Trooper*'s officers, Lieutenant Lancaster, recognised her. "Are you looking for your husband?" she asked, "They've just gone out on trials." So the two ladies adjourned to a nearby hotel for some tea while they awaited the boat's return. When she did, there was no sign of ERA Gillies – so two

---

[2] Ex-U-570. She surfaced off Iceland in misty weather on 27th Aug 41 under the nose of a patrolling Hudson aircraft from No. 269 Squadron RAF. The Hudson (Sqn Ldr Thompson) instantly straddled the target with four depth-charges which so shook the captain and crew that it was decided to surrender without a fight. The Hudson circled the boat until a Catalina arrived to take over the watch. Later, armed trawlers arrived. They took the crew off and towed the U-boat to Iceland, where she was beached. Although the crew had destroyed all the important documents, the submarine itself gave the Navy important information about the boat's capabilities. This included a fresh-water making plant and superb optics. Subsequently, it was found that there was hardly anything wrong with the boat, except for the loss of some control systems, so the surprise had led to panic and surrender. Used in RN for anti-submarine training but, apart from the technical knowledge gleaned from her, she was something of a liability for her crew. Usually flew a very large White Ensign! The *Graph* broke her tow and ran aground on Islay, West of Scotland on 20th Mar 44. Later salvaged and scrapped, after depth-charge trials were made on her hull.

sailors offered to row them out to *Trooper* to look for him. They clambered aboard, only for Nessie to be told Allison was away to Dunoon! The sailors obligingly rowed them back ashore, where Nessie went to another hotel to see if he was there, only to be told by an old man coming out that "That's no' a place fer you, lassie!" Finally, she met up with him, already aboard a lorry that was indeed about to depart for Dunoon. The couple bed and breakfasted in a croft house that in Nessie's words was "...a dump – and the bed was damp." Later on, she would climb the hills at the back of Arrochar to watch, while *Trooper* underwent her trials in the loch.

11.09.42 On Range. Salvo of 8 fired. No.11 fired accidentally.
12.09.42 On Range. 1626 No.10 [fired].
13.09.42 Loading mines
14.09.42 Laying mines. 1056 ex 1 and 2 tubes during run. 1120 ex 1 and 2. 1156 ex 3 and 4 tubes. 1229 ex 5 and 6 tubes.
15.09.42 Laying mines.
16.09.42 Torpedoes. 1629 fired No.11.
17.09.42 Arrochar to Holy Loch. Film party aboard for sound recording, etc.

Nessie Gillies remembers hearing about this film party. What the film was for has unfortunately proved impossible to discover, as no trace of it seems to remain.

18.09.42 Holy Loch to AFD VII [Admiralty Floating Dock].
                 1000 Pumping of dock started. Changed propellers. Shifted ballast.
19.09.42 Kames Bay to Holy Loch. 0855 dock flooded. Embarked 3 propellers.
                 1107 alongside FORTH. Disembarked props.
20.09.42 Holy Loch to Cumbraes, Fairlie and back.
                 1030 Embarked gunnery trials party. Guns crew closed up.
                 1042 Opened fire.
                 1048 Ceased firing.
                 1050 Trial complete.
                 1355 D/F [direction finder] calibration.
21.09.42 Holy Loch to Loch Goil and back. Noise trials. [Dived 8 times!]
                 1846 Moored hd. to stern outbd. TUNA[3].
22.09.42 Holy Loch to Inchmarnock Water and back. Attacking exercises.

---

[3] Also a Scotts-built boat. She launched Operation Frankton (Cockleshell Heroes), in December 42. Sank German s/m *U644* north-west of Narvik 7th Apr 43. She survived the war and was scrapped in June 1946

1447 Deep dive 300 ft. 10ft seam leaking in PO's [Petty Officers'] mess.

23.09.42 Holy Loch to Inchmarnock and Loch Ranza.

0915 rv BREDA[4]. Attacking ex.

2120 rv Z5[5]. Commenced night alarm ex.

2330 Completed.

24.09.42 Inchmarnock to Bute Sound.

0940 rv LA CORDILIÈRE [torpedo boat]. Attacking ex.

1745 rv Z5 towing Patt VI target and L27[6].

1806 Day surface full calibre shoot .

1822 opened fire.

1824 ceased fire.

2025 Night full calibre shoot.

2038 opened fire 1 star shell 5 practice.

2045 ceased fire.

2300 To Rothesay Bay escorted by Z5.

25.09.42 Bute Sound to Rothesay Bay to Holy Loch.

0805 Secured alongside FORTH and outboard SEALION[7].

0830 GRAPH secured port side.

1550 Slipped and proceeded to starboard trot on MM.

1630 sec. Portside to FORTH outbd. P216 [SEA DOG][8] and TUNA.

26.09.42 Holy Loch [Saturday]

27.09.42 Holy Loch to Greenock and Scotts' Basin "for alterations and additions."

28.09.42 Scotts to James Watt Dock. 1045 pumping commenced.

29-30.09.42 James Watt Dock. Hands painting ship's bottom.

01-04.10.42 James Watt Dock.

0600 Dock flooding.

1015 Undocking.

---

[4] A requisitioned wooden-hulled yacht. Became a constructive loss in 1943 when 'opened up' by foreplanes of HMS/m *Proteus* during a 'Perisher' exercise.

[5] Z5 was a Dutch destroyer that was taken over and downgraded to a patrol boat. Scrapped at Troon in 1945.

[6] Built by Vickers Armstrong in 1919, she was used for training duties in home waters throughout the war. Scuttled off the coast of Canada in 1945 as an A/S [anti-submarine] target.

[7] Based in Mediterranean 1934-39. Home waters at start of war. Sank German freighter *August Leonhardt*. Sank 3320-ton ship SW of Norway 4th Aug 1940. Transferred to 6th Flotilla, Blyth, late 1940. 1941 Arctic. Sank two small ships W of Norway 1st and 5th Feb 1941. Sank small ship N of Norway 5th Dec 41. Acted as marker submarine for Operation Anklet, raid on Lofoten Islands, Norway Dec 41. 1943 A/S training. 3rd March 1945 scuttled as Asdic target off Isle of Arran.

[8] Originally P66. Survived the war and was broken up at Troon 1948.

1200 Secured in Scott's to ROYALIST [light cruiser, built by Scotts].

06-27.10.42 At Scotts.

It seems almost certain that this was when three large containers were fitted to *Trooper*'s casing, one for'ard and two aft of the conning tower. Allison Gillies did not hesitate, when I asked him if he knew where these tanks had been fitted. "Scotts," he said at once. He also thought they had been made in Scotts' boiler shop. Both would be completely logical, especially in view of the fact that this period of three weeks has no record at all about what the boat was doing. The purpose of the containers was extremely hush-hush, as will be seen.

28.10.42 1020 Slipped ex Scotts to Holy Loch. Helensburgh DG [Degaussing] Range.

1125 trial completed.

1215 Swinging compasses.

1430 to Ardanaddam DG wiping berth.

1515 commenced DG wiping.

1800 wiping completed.

1915 sec. Outbd. P312 [TRESPASSER][9] on FORTH.

29.10.42 Holy Loch

0907 S.Ø Measured Mile 077° Gyro 3° low.

0914 dived.

0928 surfaced.

0949 dived.

0958 60 ft.

1000 PD [periscope depth]

1003 surfaced.

1010 a/c 195°.

1015 HE.

1017 dived.

1038 surfaced.

1038 sec. Port side on FORTH.

1210 THUNDERBOLT[10] secs. stbd side.

---

[9] Operated in Far East from 1944. Broken up at Gateshead.

[10] *Thunderbolt* was the name given to the ex-*Thetis*, which had sunk on her trials with the loss of 99 lives and was subsequently raised and repaired.

1313   hands embarking torpedoes.
30.10.42 Holy Loch. Hands embarking torpedoes.
31.10.42 Holy Loch. Hands embarking stores.

This log ends here and there is not another entry extant until April 1943. However, *Thunderbolt*'s log for November has survived so it is possible to follow the story of the intervening time from her perspective, which, it may fairly be assumed, much resembled that of *Trooper* and *P311*. All three boats were about to take part in a new and very secret type of operation, training for which would take place in remote Scottish sea lochs. They were to carry out the first British operation involving 'human torpedoes' or chariots.

* * *

On the night of 20th-21st December 1941, the Italians, using two-man craft officially designated as 'Siluro a Lenta Corsa', slow-running torpedoes, but familiarly known to those who were involved with them as *maiale*, or 'pigs', had a spectacular success, severely damaging the tanker *Sagona* and the destroyer HMS *Jervis*, as well as, more damaging psychologically perhaps, the battleships HMS *Valiant* and HMS *Queen Elizabeth* in the harbour at Alexandria.

An immediate result of this bold action was a note from Winston Churchill to General Sir Hastings Ismay, Secretary to the Chiefs of Staff Committee, asking what was being done to emulate the Italian feat and why Britain was not in the lead in this type of warfare. Ismay passed the note on to Vice-Admiral Sir Max Horton, Flag Officer Submarines. In April 1942, Horton sent for 45-year old Commander W R 'Tiny' Fell, a submariner and old acquaintance, and told him to "Go away and build me a Human Torpedo."

Fell worked like a demon and by September 1942 had not only built chariots that worked but had trained crews to man them. He had been given command of HMS *Titania* in June 1942, for use as his base for training charioteers. She was a World War I vintage submarine depot ship that had been based at Rothsay and as well as being

Fell's depot ship, she could also be used as a target for the chariots to practise attacking.

Early on, Fell had joined up with Commander Geoffrey Sladen. Sladen had been the commanding officer of the submarine *Trident*, which, during a highly successful patrol in Arctic waters, seriously damaged the German heavy cruiser *Prinz Eugen* off the coast of Norway on 23rd February 1942. He had also shared his accommodation with a reindeer calf that the Russians had presented to the boat when she left Murmansk, where they had been based for a time! On relinquishing command of *Trident* he had been posted to HMS *Dolphin* at Gosport, where he was working on a flexible underwater diving suit that used a closed-circuit oxygen breathing system similar to the Davis Submarine Escape Apparatus [DSEA]. The Sladen Suit, prototype of all subsequent British frogmen's apparel, was to be irreverently nicknamed 'The Clammy Death Suit' because wearing it was never a very pleasant experience, while the closed-circuit pure oxygen breathing system carried ever-present dangers from oxygen poisoning – colloquially known to chariot crews as Oxygen Pete.

Sladen and Fell both worked on the early chariots at Gosport. Recruiting of men to become charioteers was begun and initial training carried out in a lake at nearby Horsea. This was not only rather unrealistic but rather too public, so the whole chariot business was moved up to north-west Scotland, first to Loch Erisort, known as HZD, a sea-loch that penetrates well into the land mass of the Isle of Lewis in the Outer Hebrides, then, because of the uncertain weather there, a move was made to the more sheltered Loch Cairnbawn, or HHZ, in Sutherland. In these places, Fell trained the chariot crews and perfected their techniques.

As proof that interest in these activities was being taken at the very highest level, a secret memo from the First Lord, A V Alexander, to Prime Minister Churchill states:

"Training of 32 officers and 35 ratings is taking place from *Titania* at Port [H]ZD.

Six chariots and crews will be ready at the end of September [1942] and 14 operational models ready by the end of October. All crews will be trained by mid-November 42.

Containers to carry the chariots are being constructed and submarines prepared."

It goes on to say that an order for a further 24 chariots has been placed, for delivery in early 1943; that an improved design is being investigated and that air transport of chariots is also being investigated, then goes on to state the position regarding X-craft.

The first operation to use chariots began on 28th October and did not involve submarines. Captain Leif Larsen set off in his fishing boat *Arthur* – which had been operating as part of the famous 'Shetland Bus,' whose fishing vessels made many hazardous North Sea journeys to and from occupied Norway – with two chariots and their crews aboard, in an attempt to sink the *Tirpitz,* then lying in Trondhjemsfjord. The operation failed because of something quite unforeseen. When *Arthur* reached Norwegian waters, the chariots were hoisted outboard for towing below the boat so that the Germans would not see them. Very unfortunately, a storm blew up and after they had been towed for some time, the shackles pulled out from the noses of the warheads and the chariots plunged to the bottom in 100 fathoms of water. *Arthur* was scuttled and the boat's crew and all but one of the charioteers managed to escape to neutral Sweden, from where they eventually returned to Scotland.

The chariots, with their limited range, required to be transported to the vicinity of their targets. The system that had been tried using the *Arthur* had all too clearly failed. The system used so successfully by the Italians involved stowing their chariots in containers mounted on the deck of a submarine. Commander Prince Valerio Borghese, in his book *Sea Devils,* describes how his command, the 620-ton *Scirè* was modified to carry three *maiale*: "[T]hree steel cylinders had been placed on deck (two aft and one forward), having the same pressure resistance as the submarines themselves, and designed for carrying two-man torpedoes; the gun was removed, since there was now no room for it; further modifications were introduced in connection with the ventilation of the batteries of the two-man torpedoes and the flooding and exhaust systems of the cylinders themselves." It seemed sensible for the British to do the same and to this end Fell had acquired the use of an old L-class submarine, L23[11], and had her fitted with a container for his men to practice unloading their craft from.

Curiously, Fell devotes only two brief paragraphs in his book, *The Sea Our Shield*, to this next stage in chariot development: "Training was resumed with new and old crews and a greatly improved Chariot was built and tried out. Chariots were now embarked on board parent submarines in large cylindrical containers on deck," he relates, "and we could now get craft close to enemy targets that were safe from attack from conventional submarines, but not from our human torpedoes."

The chariots themselves were two-man, were 22ft 3in long, displaced one and a half tons and their nose section was a 600 lb Torpex explosive charge. They had a top speed of 4 knots with a range of 16 nautical miles at that speed and slightly more at reduced speed. Altogether thirty-four of the Mk I's were built.

The containers on the submarines were 24ft 2in long and had an exterior height of 5ft 4in. The chariots sat on wheeled bogeys inside, securely strapped down until required. In order to counter the weight and buoyancy of the containers, 9½ tons of ballast had to be added to *Trooper*'s keel, for her three, with 3½ tons being required for boats carrying two. In addition, the boats' quick-diving Q-tanks had to be kept filled with water. Ten containers were built, of which three were fitted to *Trooper*, two each to *P311* and *Thunderbolt* and one each to *L23* and *Saracen*. The unwieldy containers gave the submarines a greatly enlarged silhouette, made them 'tender' to handle laterally and "seriously detracted from their seaworthiness."

---

[11] L23 was built by Vickers, Barrow but completed at Chatham Dockyard and launched in 1919. Having been used for training throughout the war, she was sold for scrap in 1946 but foundered while on tow off Nova Scotia.

In September 1942, one chariot was sent by Fell to Malta for trials. It was carried in the container fitted to HMS/m *Saracen*. Fell makes no mention of this and there is nothing about it in the boat's logs or patrol reports but Captain G W G Simpson, who was Captain (S) Ten at Malta at the time, mentions it, as does Admiral Arthur Hezlet. It will be recalled that *Saracen* was present in the Clyde on 29th August, and that *Trooper* tied up alongside her that day. However it seems likely that she did not embark her chariot – and possibly not her container – until shortly before leaving Gibralter for Malta on 9th October, having previously conducted a 10-day patrol, between 17th and 24th September, from and back to the Rock.

Fell's last mention of chariots is inexplicably cryptic; the more so as the working up and training of their crews had dominated activity at Loch Cairnbawn for months. "I sent eight well-trained crews with their craft out to Geoff Sladen, who was now in the Mediterranean, and in 1943 they carried out two brilliant and altogether successful attacks."

One of those men was the late Sub-Lt Rodney Dove, RNVR, DSO, whose comments qualify the phrase 'well-trained':

"...there are a couple of points about our training that I think are worth mention. The first is that in 1942 the whole chariot/human torpedo weaponry and use was being invented; the concept, the operational procedures, the viability of sending men into enemy harbours riding these extraordinary "under-water motor bikes" carrying a warhead containing 600 lbs of amatol plus a detonation time clock and putting it under a ship; and somehow, with a lot of luck, bringing the crew back out again. The training was being put together at the same time as the weapon and tactics were being invented. Inevitably, the training was rudimentary, experimental and in some respects inadequate.... I don't think our training was very good. I personally made several terrible booboos in my training, and in hindsight I realise that I was quite inadequate as an operational charioteer. Fortunately I seemed to be lucky."[12]

* * *

HUSH - MOST SECRET   OUT

HUSH – MOST SECRET.   MESSAGE.   1518A/18th October. Out.

Date 18.10.42

To: -   F.O.C.N.A. 10.
Repeated C. in C. Mediterranean   387 B3.
        V.A. Malta.   656.
         S.1.
         S.10
         F.O.S.452.

NAVAL CYPHER (6 Way)

From Admiralty.

HUSH. THUNDERBOLT, P.311 and TROOPER fitted with large special containers on the upper deck leave United Kingdom for Malta without calling at Gibraltar. For security reasons it is undesirable that these submarines should either pass through the Straits during daylight or be escorted. Subject to your concurrence it is proposed that submarines should arrive in position 350 degs. Spartel 10 miles at specified times and proceed through Straits on surface. Expect submarines will pass through Straits as follows (dates are approximate and will be confirmed later).

       THUNDERBOLT   19th November
       P.311 and TROOPER   23rd November

         1518A/18

         for D.O.D.(F)

1st Lord
1st S.L. (2)
D.F.S.L.
4th S.L. (3)
V.C.N.S.
A.C.N.S.(H)

---

[12] Rodney Dove *pers. comm.*

A.C.N.S.(F) (2)
A.C.N.S.(T)
A.C.N.S.(W)
N.A. 1st S.L.
D.O.D.(H)
D.O.D.(F)
D.of P. (2)
D.N.I.
D.D.I.C.   Admiral Blake
D. of P.(0)   Hd. Of M. (14)
Duty Capt.   C.C.O. (2)
D.S.D.   D. of L.D.

This highly secret operational notification and distinguished distribution list – right up to the First Lord of the Admiralty and the First Sea Lord – indicate something of the importance that was being attached to getting the submarines and their precious cargoes safely to Malta and to the scene of the operation to follow.

It is certain that most of the time *Trooper* spent, after she sailed from Holy Loch in early November until she received sailing orders on 11th November, was spent training with the chariots. Confirmation that Cairnbawn is where she went comes from the diary kept by ERA Peter Forbes. He joined the boat at the last minute, getting a 'pier-head jump' to replace someone who went sick. His very first entry, on 5th November, states "Left Dunoon to do trial runs with our new invention – two-man torpedoes," and on 7th November he writes "Arrived at Loch Craigenbaum [*sic*], north-west coast of Scotland. Very quiet and out of the way spot. Our aim was to get through the defences of the new battleship *Howe*." [This of course meant the charioteers, not the submarine.] *Howe* was present for three days. She was brand new, only being completed on 29th August 1942, and remained with the Home Fleet until 1943. It is a measure of the importance being attached to forthcoming chariot operations that a valuable battleship should be 'lent' in this way, for the chariot crews to practice attacking. *Trooper*'s log for this period is missing but *Thunderbolt*'s records what must have been very similar activities on the part of all three boats. It begins on 1st November:

01.11.42 Holy Loch to HHZ.
0105 At sea.
1135 secured alongside TITANIA.
1415 to buoy.
1441 Commenced exercises.
1625 Exercises completed.
1630 Slipped buoy. [The exercises must have been made while secured to the buoy]
1710 Alongside TITANIA.
1845 Slipped.
1903 Secured to buoy.
1906 Commenced exercises.
2100 Rounds correct.
2224 Completed exercises.

02.11.42 0800 Hands turned to.
1400 Slipped, on MM's.
1426 Sec. to buoy commenced exercises.
1625 Completed exercises. Slipped to go alongside TITANIA.
1700 Secured alongside.
1858 Slipped and proceeded to buoy on MM's.
1917 Sec. to buoy.
1935 Commenced exercises.
2100 Rounds correct.
2300 Completed exercises.

03.11.42 0800 Hands turned to.
0810 Slipped buoy and proceeded to TITANIA.
0835 Secured alongside.
0907 Slipped and proceeded on MM's to buoy.
0934 Secured to buoy.
1845 Commenced independent exercises.
1945 Disembarked landing party.
2100 Rounds correct.
2330 Landing party returned.
2345 Completed exercises. [Was 'landing party' a euphemistic reference to chariots? DRG]

04.11.42 0800 Hands turned to.

1020 Commenced special exercise.

1100 Completed special exercise.

1315 Slipped buoy and proceeded on MM's alongside TITANIA.

1345 Sec. alongside TITANIA port side.

2100 Rounds correct.

2208 Duty watch turned to, doubled up springs, put on extra head and stern wires [There had been a gale warning at 2200 hrs].

0128 Commenced exercises.

0317 Completed Exercises.

05.11.42 0800 Hands turned to.

1821 Commenced special exercises.

2100 Rounds correct.

06.11.42 0800 Hands turned to.

1017 Slipped and proceeded on MM's to buoy.

1045 Secured to buoy.

2100 Rounds correct.

07.11.42 0800 Hands turned to.

1750 *P311* came alongside.

1755 *P311* secured to starboard side.

2100 Rounds correct.

08.11.42 0800 Harbour stations. Slipped and proceeded on MM's.

0900 Secured to *TROOPER.*

0910 Slipped and proceeded on MM's.

0945 Secured alongside TITANIA.

1310 Slipped and proceeded on MM's.

1341 Secured to TITANIA. Bows to stern for embarking stores.

1930 Completed embarking stores.

2100 Rounds correct.

09.11.42 0800 Hands turned to.

0845 Slipped and proceeded on MM's to buoy.

0917 Secured to Buoy.

2100 Rounds correct.

10.11.42 0800 Hands turned to, prepared for sea.

1052 slipped and proceeded on ME's courses and speeds as requisite for leaving Edrachillis Bay.

The place of departure on her sailing orders is given as co-ordinates: 58° 15' North 05° 04' West. A look at Chart 2720, *St Kilda to Cape Wrath including the North Minch*, shows that position to be HHZ, the wartime code letters for Loch Cairnbawn. In Gaelic its name is Loch a'Chàirn Bhàin, meaning Loch of the White Cairn. Thereafter *Thunderbolt* headed down the Minch, recording sighting the Shiant Isles, Vaternish Point, Neist Point and on to reach the Mull of Kintyre by 0535 on 11th November. She was escorted as far as the Bishop Rock by the venerable 1920's vintage destroyer, HMS *Cutty Sark*, detaching from her at 1808 on the 12th. At 1650 on the 20th, she transferred documents to the escort destroyer HMS *Avonvale* and at 2000 "took station astern of escort" in position 36°00' N 5°26' W for passage through the Straits of Gibraltar. Rather surprisingly perhaps, depending upon what exactly they were, she "commenced independent exercises" at 1755 in position 38° 56.4' N 2° 57.5' W. Then, on the 28th at 0958 "Sighted escort HMS *Blyth* [a minesweeper]. 1045 On station astern of BLYTH. 1307 Secured alongside *P247* [*Saracen*] in Lazaretto Creek." The passages of *P311* and *Trooper*, following two days later, must have been very similar.

It is clear, to revert briefly to Loch Cairnbawn, that from their mention in *Thunderbolt*'s log, *P311 and Trooper* were both at HHZ at this time as well. The photograph of *Thunderbolt* alongside HMS *Titania*, with her containers fitted, is captioned as being either in Loch Erisort or in Loch Cairnbawn, but is certainly the latter, as *Titania* was there by then. Time was short and all three boats had to load their chariots for the passage to Malta. Intensive practice for the charioteers was continuing and, although they would have had the benefit of using the container fitted to *L23*, this was the first opportunity for the submarines' crews to try out the techniques required for launching chariots from their own containers. This required the boat to surface, then for the already-dressed chariot crews to exit and don their breathing apparatus, which was too bulky to be worn while coming up through the conning tower. Members of the boat's crew opened the containers, pulled out the chariots and then

34

shut the container doors. Failure to shut a door could have resulted in a container flooding when the boat later dived, with fatal consequences[13]. The submarine next had to trim down to the point where the chariots could be floated off. It was a hazardous procedure at the best of times and in a rough sea both difficult and dangerous. It also meant the submarine spending a fraught 15 minutes – or more – on the surface in hostile waters. Lt Dickie Greenland maintains that he *never* trained with the submarines, either in Cairnbawn or at Malta and in this he is supported by Sub-Lt Dove. While one hesitates to doubt their memories, it does seem extraordinary that there would not have been rehearsals of the launching procedure.

Trooper and *P311* received their sailing orders, marked MOST SECRET from HMS *Titania*, dated 11th November. They were further marked "To be destroyed when complied with; <u>Not</u> to be allowed to fall into the hands of the enemy." The boats were to have as escort *La Capricieuse*[14] as far as the Bishop Rock. She would then leave them and return to Holy Loch. The little convoy was to depart at noon the following day, to arrive 10 miles south of Bishop Rock Light at 1800 on the 14th and from there the two boats would proceed independently to Malta. *Thunderbolt*, of course, was ahead of them. Unlike *Trooper* and *P311*, which were both brand-new, she had been on active service since 1940, although in August she had completed a long refit at Devonport.

Special Instructions appended to the orders gave specific directions. *P311* was ordered to proceed, diving by day, to a series of en route positions, the last of which she was to reach "by 2000/18" and then to make her passage through the Straits of Gibraltar "probably in the hours of darkness thence submerged by day to Malta." *Trooper's* orders were identical, with the exception of the en route positions, which were slightly different and the timing for reaching the last one, which was "by

---

[13] Pamela Mitchell, in her book *Chariots Under the Sea,* describes an experiment whereby a chariot was launched underwater, but it is unclear if this involved a container – a flooded container would hold 12 tons of water!

[14] *La Capricieuse* was a modern French mine-sweeper, launched in 1939. She was seized by the Royal Navy on 3rd July 1940, while docked at Portsmouth and was operated by them throughout the war. She was returned to France on 6th June 1945 and continued in service until September 1964.

0300/19." The Instructions ended, as had *Thunderbolt*'s: "Every effort is to be made to prevent *P311* and *Trooper* being sighted on the surface in order to prevent cargo being discovered. Full use must be made of RDF[15] to avoid aircraft."

The codeword for passage to Malta for all three vessels was PRINCIPAL, the same as that to be given to the operation that the boats were to undertake, delivering the chariots to positions where they could attack shipping in Italian harbours.

Some excerpts from Peter Forbes's diary add a little flesh to the bare bones of official communications.

12th November 1942.

Left for Malta, no stops on the way, where we are to operate from to do our "Jeeps"[16], as we call our runs. Immediately we got under way, the captain told us that these "Jeeps" had had a successful attack against the German battleship *Tirpitz* in a Norwegian fiord. [Alas this was untrue, as Operation 'Title' had failed, as previously noted, when the two chariots, being towed beneath a fishing boat, became detached.]

14th November.

Hugging the coast on the surface. We must be near Land's End now. Still on the surface even though the escort has left us. Trip to take us 14 days.

15th November.

Dived all day today as we are within range of the enemy. Had practice night alarm last night.

---

[15]RDF stands for Radio Direction Finding – the precursor of Radar.
[16] Charioteers invariably referred to their two-man craft as Jeeps, after the character Wimpy, in Popeye cartoons, who made a noise 'jeep-jeep-jeep'. The original reason for this is now obscure, though chariot propellers apparently made a similar sound.

17th November.

RDF has fallen over [become unserviceable], we were relying a lot on it too. It may take longer as we were planning to do three days on the surface but must dive all day now.

19th November.

A week out now, in the danger area, said to be infested with U-boats.

20th November.

We are in Portuguese waters now, close to shore, we saw the lights of Lisbon last night. Liable to be interned if we are caught. Ahead of schedule – going slow.

21st November.

Still on dive all day routine, our fresh food is nearing exhaustion so we will have to revert to dehydrated foodstuffs now. Crash dive last night, enemy aircraft about.

23rd November.

Escort took us past Gibraltar, we were dived to avoid our tanks, which we keep our "Jeeps" in, from being seen.

The Passage Report forwarded by Captain (S), 10th Submarine Flotilla, G W G Simpson, to Captain (S) First Submarine Flotilla HMS *Medway II*, added little, simply stating that *Trooper* had left the UK on the 12th and "made an uneventful passage. The escort was met and passage through the Straits of Gibraltar took place without incident." Simpson does go on to say that the boat had been ordered, when approaching Pantellaria on 29th, to remain in the Tyrrhenian Sea until further orders as the northern route "through QBB.255" was believed to have been compromised. After dark on the 30th November, *Trooper* was ordered to make the passage of the Sicilian Channel "by the deep water route passing 10 miles west of Pantellaria during daylight of 1st December." *Trooper* arrived at Malta on the afternoon of 2nd December 1942.

ERA Peter Forbes's diary for 28th however, mentions diving "through enemy minefield near Pantellaria, Italian fortified island near Malta. Safe enough to dive through mines ordinarily but, with tanks on, it is very dangerous". And on 30th "…. then at night Captain decided to charge full speed on top of the minefield, for the rest of the night. Our luck held – thank God".

P311 had sailed on the same day as *Trooper*. According to the *Report of Proceedings* submitted by her CO to the Captain (S) "The passage was uneventful." Her Captain, Lt Cdr R D Cayley, mentions sighting fishing vessels on 15th November and again on 20th. On the 27th an unidentified flying boat was noted, while on the 28th a submarine was spotted on the surface at 0245 "Probably HMS *Tribune*".[17] By the 29th they were off Maritimo [Isola Marittimo, Sicily], where "at 0835 sighted 40 Troop Transport Aircraft. Course 180°" and later that day, "at 1600 sighted Periscope. Established S/ST [ship to ship transmission] communication with HMS *Una*."[18] *P311* arrived in Malta in the afternoon of 30th November, two days earlier than *Trooper*.

* * *

Commander Fell, as has been mentioned, by his own account had sent "eight well-trained crews" of charioteers to Malta. Eleven officers and fifteen ratings had sailed for Gibraltar, spirits a little dampened, no doubt, by the death of Sub-Lieutenant Jack Grogan SANF (V) [South African Naval Forces (Volunteer)], during one of the practice attacks on the *Howe* a few days earlier. From there they had flown to Malta. Cdr Geoff Sladen was already there. After a tremendous party to celebrate their arrival, the men were all set to a vigorous training programme, in spite of the difficulties presented by the sub-standard accommodation and limited variety of food that was all that was available in Malta. The island's worst times were past but life there was still no sinecure.

---

[17] *Tribune* was another Scotts-built boat. She survived the war to be scrapped in 1947.
[18] *Una* was launched at HMDY Chatham in 1941, had successes in the Mediterranean and survived to be scrapped in 1949.

Little is recorded of those weeks before Christmas 1942. Off-duty, opportunities for recreation were limited and to avoid his keyed-up and impatient crews getting up to too much mischief, Sladen kept them hard at work. The three submarines arrived shortly after the charioteers. Their containers were hidden under canvas covers, upon which the word "Petrol" was stencilled in large letters, to disguise their true purpose.

The boats were heavily involved in training with the charioteers. Peter Forbes again:

> "During our stay in Malta we were doing trial runs with our "Jeeps" almost every night; by the account of things it is not going to be an easy job either. We are all wondering what harbour we are going into. We assume that it is to sink units of the Italian fleet lying in harbour."

And from *Thunderbolt*'s log, after the week from 1st to 7th December, when she was "in Lazaretto Creek," then moved on the 8th to secure alongside *P311* at 'U4' buoy, shows that she frequently carried out "independent exercises" right through until 27th December. During this period, *Trooper*'s sister ship HMS/m *Traveller*, operating out of Beirut and commanded by Lt Drummond St Clair Ford in place of her usual CO, Lt Michael St John, who was ill, was sent to reconnoitre in the Gulf of Taranto. This was mainly to assess the possibility of making a successful chariot attack there. Ominously, she failed to return, presumed to have hit a mine about 4th December. "This sort of thing dampens our spirits," wrote Peter Forbes laconically.

Captain (S) Ten, the commander of the 10th Submarine Flotilla, was the redoubtable G W G "Shrimp" Simpson. He had fought his boats all through the long period of Malta's battering by the combined might of the Luftwaffe and the Regia Aeronautica, working tirelessly to ease the almost impossible conditions for his crews when they came back to port and enduring agonies of spirit whenever a boat was lost. He knew all the skippers well and Lt Cdr Cayley, captain of *P311*, was a particular friend. Simpson describes the arrival of the three submarines:

"It was good to see John Wraith and Dick Cayley back again and Crouch was a splendid man whose leadership had restored the ill-fated *Thetis*....into the confident offensive *Thunderbolt*.

I met the effervescent roly-poly figure of Cayley on the landing steps. 'Hello, sir,' he said. 'Looks as if you've had the housebreakers in! It's good to be home again!'.....

Harmonica Dick, as he was known throughout the service, searched in his uniform pocket, produced his mouth organ and after a few bars said, 'Let us now praise famous men and our fathers who begat us. Gosh it's good to be back, sir."

Lt Johnny Wraith was another of Simpson's 'old hands,' having been in command of HMS/m *Upright* since the middle of June 1941 until she arrived back in the UK for a refit ten months later, and scoring some notable successes. Simpson said this about the man who was now CO of *Trooper*:

"Lieutenant John S Wraith appeared, on first acquaintance, to be an average, rather shy, officer, who seemed self-deprecating and possibly lacking in self-confidence. This was the veneer to a very modest man with a great sense of humour who in action was entirely self-confident. I well remember how, in the early hours of 13th December 1941, in command of *Upright*, Wraith carried out a night attack on an escorted convoy in the Gulf of Taranto. He sank two new sister ships, only a few months from the builder's yard, on their first laden voyage, both of 6,335 tons. His typical explanation was, 'They simply committed suicide, sir. Just ran into my torpedoes!'"

Unlike Cayley and Wraith, Lt Cdr Cecil Crouch had never been part of the 10th Flotilla. He came to the captaincy of *Thunderbolt* as a seasoned submariner from HMS/m *Swordfish* and by the time of Operation 'Principal' his new command had become a highly successful one. She had opened her score by sinking the Italian submarine *Tarantini*; spent a spell as convoy escort operating out of Halifax; picked up 43 survivors from the sinking of the ss *Guelma* near Funchal and completed a number of Mediterranean patrols out of Alexandria before being sent back to Devonport for her refit, prior to taking part in 'Principal.'

Now Simpson was about to send these three very experienced men off on a type of mission never before undertaken by the Royal Navy. He was all too aware of the dangers the boats faced on their way and for that reason sent the seasoned Cayley away first, to make the passage through the Sicilian minefields by a route he had pioneered months before. The other two would follow as soon as *P311* signalled she was safely clear. There was an added complication, in that the RAF had reported considerable anti-submarine activity west of Marittimo Island and later that a convoy had sailed from Cagliari roads.

Thus on 28th December, *P311* left Malta, to be followed on 29th by *Thunderbolt* and *Trooper,* taking a total of seven chariots to their allotted tasks on this novel first operation, code-named 'Principal.' Again, *Thunderbolt*'s log gives a glimpse of the departure:

> 29.12.42 1700 Harbour stations.
>
> 1720 Slipped from buoys and proceeded to sea, helm, engines to CO's orders.
>
> 1735 Cleared boom, entered swept channel in station astern of HMS *Trooper* 1 ml. Var. courses through swept channel.
>
> 1745 Both engine clutches in. 420 revs ordered. Patrol routine.
>
> 1940 Cleared swept channel. Co. set 296°.
>
> 2047 Commenced zigzag 20° each side main co. every 5 mins.

The extreme caution being exercised by Simpson in getting these very vulnerable boats to their positions shows in the next day's entry:

> 30.12.42 0130 Sighted [Isola di] Linosa brg. 230°. Approx. posn. 36° 08'N 13°13.5'E
>
> 1227 a/co. [altered course] as ordered in route orders.
>
> 1310 a/co. as ordered by W/T. <u>Operation delayed</u>.

> 1721 a/co to CO's orders. Var. courses thereon awaiting orders to proceed.
>
> 1750 Up to 30 ft.

Trooper was actually being held in position 36°15'N 11°45'E, while *Thunderbolt* was held at 36°10'N 12°10'E. They were still dodging about early the following morning as *Thunderbolt*'s log shows:

> 31.12.42 Various courses to CO's orders maintaining posn., speed etc., S of Pantellaria.
>
> 0200 Proceed on passage in accordance with W/T orders.

Peter Forbes recorded what was known 'below decks': "Left Malta to do our secret job with our two-man torpedoes. Three submarines fitted out same as us, we are all going to the same place we think.....[later] Our aim is to enter Palermo Bay and attack shipping in the port." His entry for 31st December highlighted what must have been a point of extreme frustration for all the CO's and crews: "Last day of year. Sighted Italian convoy [perhaps the one reported by the RAF as being at Cagliari and *Thunderbolt*'s original target], easy target but Captain has his orders to leave everything alone, we are after bigger game. We are close by Sicily now." Because of the possibility of hazarding the whole operation, orders had been given forbidding anything except a capital ship to be attacked. There was a practical point to this as well, for with two, or in *Trooper*'s case, three, containers on their casings, the boats were somewhat unstable. Had one or more containers been ruptured by a severe depth-charge attack, the boat would have been anchored to the sea-bed by the extra weight of water, so the risk was very great.

The original plan called for Cayley to proceed to a position off La Maddalena, in the north of Sardinia, where air reconnaissance had shown two 8-inch gun cruisers lay, there to launch *P311*'s chariots; Crouch was to take *Thunderbolt* to Cagliari, where a convoy was reported as assembling, with Palermo as an alternate should the convoy have sailed, while Wraith and *Trooper* made for Palermo. The original date set for the attacks was the night of 1st/2nd January 1943. At 0130 on 31st December, Cayley had duly reported back as arranged, after passing safely through the minefields. He gave his position as 38° 10′ N. 11° 30′ E. This was well north of the reported anti-submarine activity, which had in any case dispersed by this time. Simpson therefore signalled to the other two boats to continue their passage:

MOST SECRET.   MESSAGE.   IN.

From Capt. (S) 10.   Date: 31.12.42

Recd: 0425

NAVAL CODE '02' BY W/T

Addressed THUNDERBOLT, TROOPER, repeated C. in C. Mediterranean, N.C.X.P., S/M's on Patrol

<u>IMMEDIATE</u>

P.311 is up to schedule. Comply with my 1237/30th. Consider you should be free of torpedo boats patrols but ASV aircraft and E-boats may menace. When past position 038 degs. 31′ 011 degs. 25′ make signal "arrived" addressed to me.

0320A/31

Because of the delays the boats' passages had been subject to, the assault on Palermo was postponed for twenty-four hours, to the night of 2nd/3rd January 1943. *Thunderbolt* was prowling about in the region of Isola di Ustica early on the morning of 2nd:

02.01.43 0557 Ustica brg.166° 12.5 mls (approx) a/co. toward position ordered.
0621 Diving stns.
0623 Dived.
0627 At 60ft. Watch diving. Watch diving at 60 ft, coming up to 30 ft. for W/T routines.
1116 Garazzi Pt. (Ustica) L.H. 079° 3mls. a/co.
1200 In position 325° 6 mls from ordered position.
1600 C. Falconara (Ustica) 332° 12 mls. a/co.
1700 Up to 30 ft.
1833 Diving stns.

1848 Surfaced.

1852 Running charge to stbd, standng chg port. A/co for run in to position for operation

1854 Patrol routine

Trooper also was moving in towards the target area. The wind on the approach had been nor'west, Force 3 to 4, with a lumpy sea running [according to *Thunderbolt*]. The situation for her charioteers was about to become very much less comfortable than in the warmth of the engine room. When Sub-Lt R G Dove RNVR and L/S Freel, his number two, climbed with some difficulty up the conning tower, fully kitted out in their Sladen suits, they found a dirty night awaiting them. It was pitch black, with a Force 4 to 5 offshore wind creating a nasty chop on the sea. The submarine was "bouncing up and down like a yo-yo on a short string" as they made their way forward using 'one hand for the ship and one for themselves.' Spray was being flung over the bows in sheets. Dove graphically describes what happened next:

"[The] launch of the chariots from the deck of *Trooper* was the crucial first step in our chariot operation. In *Trooper* there were five pairs of charioteers, that is, three pairs to man the three chariots and two pairs to help in dressing these operational crews. The operational pairs were Lt Cook and AB Worthy, Sub Lt Stevens and Ldg Seaman Carter, and me – Sub Lt Dove and Ldg Seaman Freel. *Trooper* was about five miles off the harbour of Palermo, not fully on the surface but sufficiently to have the upper casing deck a few feet above the sea level. Ratings of *Trooper's* crew opened the doors of the containers and pulled out the chariots on the rails ready for launch. The drill was that the operational charioteers, dressed in their diving suits and breathing apparatus, would stand beside their respective chariots on the inboard side of them, and *Trooper* would then trim down a few feet lower in the water so that the chariots and their crews would float off into the sea and begin proceeding to the harbour entrance under their own power. We all took our positions for this to happen. This meant that, on the after casing, two operational pairs, i.e. four men, were standing between the two chariots. The idea was that one chariot and pair would float off on the port

44

side of *Trooper*, and the other on the starboard side. Freel and I were to go off the starboard. In theory, this is a fairly simple procedure.... The catch in this case was that, instead of a reasonably benign sea, there was something like half a gale blowing from a bit west of south, which would be in our faces for the journey to the harbour entrance. Moreover it created sizeable waves. When *Trooper* trimmed down, instead of the chariots and pairs gently floating off to port and starboard, a wave lifted both chariots and all four charioteers and dumped them down on the port side of *Trooper*. This, to say the least of it, was an alarming experience, especially for Freel and me, who were supposed to launch to starboard. Fortunately it was a clean dumping into the sea, and I got weaving immediately, mounting the chariot, starting the electric motor, steering for the harbour entrance five miles away, checking pressure tanks to arrive at just positive buoyancy, and so on. I did not have time to consider how ghastly the launch might have turned out to be if the wave had not been so large, and if our feet had thereby been impeded by the rail, so that the chariot crashed down on *Trooper*'s deck. It wasn't till much later that this though occurred to me."

They did not realise that their bosun's locker, situated behind the No 2's seat, and which contained all their tools, had become detached and washed overboard.

Both the other crews also got away all right. Cook had suffered dreadfully from sea-sickness during the bumpy passage and was not really in a fit state to carry out such an arduous and dangerous mission; nevertheless he would not hear of abandoning it.

Her chariots all gone and the container doors firmly shut, a no-doubt relieved Lt Wraith took *Trooper* back to the safety of deeper waters. Spending an hour on the surface not far offshore from a major enemy harbour, even on a wild pitch-black night, was not an enjoyable situation for any submarine commander.

Peter Forbes, in describing what he knew, shows how little of events the crew were sometimes aware of: "Entered the bay last night at 9.00 pm, surfaced nearly three miles from port, sat on the surface and let the "jeeps" off, this took us nearly an hour. Two submarines were there, us and *Thunderbolt*. The other one was attacking a port in Sardinia. Set off out again at full speed on donkeys [main motors]."

Meanwhile, *Thunderbolt* had almost arrived in her position:

> 2007 C. Gallo Lt. obsvd. 189° 11.2 mls.
> 2045 Engines stopped, future movements on main motors.
> 2056 Observed brkwtr lts.
> 2059 Diving stns. Operation commenced.
> 2138 In position with Diga Foranea Lt. 224° 5.0 mls a/co to close light. Main motors & helm to CO's orders throughout.
> 2201 Trimmed down.
> 2202 Launches made.
> 2216 Operation completed and a/co to retire. Full buoyancy ordered
> 2229 Patrol routine.

Thus she had rapidly and successfully sent away her two chariots, though not any more easily than her sister ship had done. After a difficult launch, Lt Greenland's and L/Sig Ferrier's craft got away into the heavy sea, her crew narrowly missing being maimed by the submarine's jumping wire, which came plunging down on them as they left the deck. The crew of the other chariot, Petty Officer Miln and A/B Simpson were washed violently off the deck as they mounted their machine. Somehow they clung on, and they too, floated free of the submarine and disappeared into the mirk, heading for Palermo. *Thunderbolt* also then retired from her exposed position and by 2315 was "zigzagging as usual" while at 2350, when she was nearly 20 miles away, her log records "Heavy flash followed by report of explosion astern" indicating success for at least one chariot.

Because of the inadvisability of keeping the big T-class submarines with their unwieldy deck cargoes hanging around for long to recover the chariots, HMS/m *Unruffled* (P46), commanded by Lt J S Stevens, DSO DSC RN had been ordered to patrol inshore off Palermo. In the event, Sub-Lt Stevens and L/S Carter, who had had great difficulty finding the entrance to Palermo harbour, followed by problems with Carter's breathing set, after some six hours in the water wisely abandoned their attack and proceeded to the rendezvous point. They were beginning to despair of being picked up when they saw the outline of *Unruffled* looming out of the dark. One can only imagine the relief they must have felt. But they were the only men to be picked up and it was only later that the fate of the rest of the Palermo crews became known.

Lt Stevens had been *Thunderbolt*'s First Lieutenant, and had stood by her at Cammel Laird's Birkenhead yard while she was metamorphosed from her former existence as the ill-fated *Thetis*. He describes what happened:

"I learned that *P46* was to act as recovery vessel for Operation 'Principal', the first time that chariots had been used in action. We sailed on December 28th, while *Thunderbolt* and her sister, *Trooper*, left with chariots and crews embarked, a day later. ... Our orders were to be stopped on the surface, in a position three miles from Palermo harbour entrance, from 0400 to 0530. In this time we were to pick up as many as possible of the charioteers, who were to scuttle their craft. ... Chariot XXIII manned by my namesake, Sub-Lieutenant H L Stevens RNVR and Chief Petty Officer Buxton, suffered a breakdown which caused them to abandon their attack. They made their way towards us, and had a lucky escape as the feeble light of their torch being flashed to seaward was barely visible. As it was, we finally recovered them ninety minutes after the deadline time when we should have started a dived withdrawal."

Further north, HMS/m *Unison* (*P43*), whose CO, Lt A R Daniell, DSC RN had been Wraith's First Lieutenant on *Upright* before getting his own command, was fulfilling the same function for recovery of *P311*'s chariots. HMS/m *Unbending* (*P37*), commanded by Lt E S Stanley, had been detailed for Cagliari but with the abandonment of that objective, was not required. There was of course, no certainty that any of the charioteers would make it back to the rendezvous points, because even if successful it was quite probable they would have to land, risking almost certain capture. In the case of the attack on La Maddalena, because of the minefields protecting the base, it was planned that the charioteers would be met on shore and taken off in folbots.

All the boats had received a signal from Simpson just after midnight as follows:

MOST SECRET.   MESSAGE.   1203A/3 Jan.

From: Captain (S) 10.   DATE: 3.1.43

NAVAL CODE (0.2) SECRET by W/T

Addressed: S/ms on patrol. Repeated Capt. (S) 8

C. in C. Mediterranean, N.C.X.F., Capt. (S) 1,

V.A. Malta

IMMEDIATE

Take following action:-

P43 move to a waiting position 090 degs. Ustica 6.

P46 if you have personnel on board withdraw to 038 degs. 40' 012 degs 40' and signal report of their operation and yours in one time pad after dark.

If you have no extra personnel proceed 038 degs. 30' 014 degs. 00' and report after dark thence proceed via Cape Milazzo northward to operate South of Naples off Bocca Piccolo.

H.M.S. THUNDERBOLT set course to pass through 038 degs. 50' 012 degs. 00' to arrive G. at 0800A. 4th. Thence by normal route to R/V with sweepers 0800A/6. [i.e. minesweepers]

H.M.S. TROOPER to follow H.M.S. THUNDERBOLT's route 24 hours later.

P311 if transfer of Kerr allowed follows 24 hours behind H.M.S.TROOPER to arrive Malta 0800A 8th January.

Off Maddalena, Lt Daniell had two collapsed folbots[18] taken out of the torpedo tubes in which they had been stowed and hoisted on deck, where they were quickly assembled.

---

[18] The folbot was a folding kayak developed in the UK pre-war. The company moved to the USA and still exists. See also account of *Trooper's* 5th War Patrol in main text.

Daniell wrote: "I decided that Derek Palmer, our fourth hand, would paddle ashore with one of our crew and two folbot canoes to contact the expected charioteers. He was to whistle or hum some bars of *Rule Britannia* at intervals to demonstrate his *bona fide*. Alas no charioteers came."

In fact it is highly doubtful if *P311* ever reached the position at which she would have launched her chariots. Cayley's signal reporting his position was the last ever heard from the submarine. Sadly, she, the gallant and kenspeckle Dick Cayley, his fine crew and the highly-trained charioteers were lost, presumed mined in the Straits of Bonifacio.

"After a few more days of suspense," wrote Peter Forbes in his diary for 7th January, "we finally arrived back in Malta. Six letters awaiting me, lovely, all from Molly [his wife]." He had noted the previous day that "According to reports a cruiser and five ships were sunk by the both of us," to which he was able to add on the 9th that "A few of the men on the "Jeeps" were killed, the two of us returned safely [i.e. *Trooper* and *Thunderbolt*] but the one that attacked the other port has not returned, presumed lost. Another T-boat."

On the 9th too, the Vice-Admiral Malta, Admiral Ralph Leatham, sent a message to the Commander in Chief Mediterranean, Admiral Andrew Cunningham, about the operation:

HUSH MOST SECRET   MESSAGE   IN

0051/9th January.

From: V.A. Malta   Date: 9.1.43

Naval Cypher I.T.P. by Cable

Addressed: C. in C. Mediterranean, Repeated N.C.X.F.,

Admiralty, Capt. S.1., Capt. S.8.

IMPORTANT

597. <u>Capt. S.10 reports</u> H.M.S. THUNDERBOLT reports operation carried out according to plan, with view to improving sea conditions launched from 3.3 miles from harbour entrance at the exact ordered time, intermittent switching on of harbour lights <u>aided</u> accurate fix wind W.S.W. force 6 but lee-way adequate.

(ii) H.M.S. TROOPER reports operation carried out according to plan except <u>half</u> hour late launching closed harbour entrance to 4.7 miles concurs with H.M.S. THUNDERBOLT re condition of sea and fixing, his chariots experienced adverse set. Both S/Ms waited to see Chariots trim <u>and</u> away then retired to pre-arranged position.

(iii) Both emphasised that although all personnel somewhat seasick on surface run in they were entirely recovered <u>and</u> <u>fully</u> confident <u>when</u> launching.

(iv) P 46 reported uneventful passage <u>to</u> <u>Ustica</u> then close Westward and <u>were</u> <u>in</u> recovery position 3.5 miles from breakwater at 0250. At 0350 sighted chariots flash, intercepted and embarked 0435, since no other in sight withdrew. Throughout this period there was no sign of activity in harbour. Between 0515 and 0535 about 6 vivid white flashes occurred in harbour P46 was withdrawn and [?] 12 miles away.

(v) Rescued personnel who abandoned attack one mile from entrance due defects confirm that those who entered harbour appeared to be undetected.

(vi) Full report including sailing orders to S/M concerned will be sent by first safe opportunity to addressees.

The story of what happened to the charioteers has been extensively written up in a number of books; nevertheless it is fitting to give a brief summary here. *Trooper's* three chariots, having all launched safely, had to battle difficult sea conditions that made the chariots hard to control and then had mixed fortunes. Stevens and Carter on Chariot XXIII, whose main target was the mv *Ankara,* had had to abort their attack as described above. The main target assigned to Rodney Dove and Freel on Chariot XVI was the 8,500-ton troop transport ss *Viminale,* with, as secondary targets for their limpet mines, three motor vessels.

Dove and Freel's attack, as described in Dove's own words, went like this:

"The strong wind delayed our timely arrival at the harbour entrance, as did an error in my pilotage which caused me to reach its protecting mole about half a mile too far west. We were therefore quite late in diving under the fifty foot deep anti-torpedo net protecting the entrance. In fact it must have been after 4:30 a.m. because the moon had already risen well above the eastern horizon, and we knew that the submarine detailed to wait five miles off to pick us up from the sea afterwards would dive and abandon its mission at 0430 moonrise. There was therefore no chance of subsequent escape.

There was a further important misery about our particular journey from *Trooper* to the harbour – or perhaps, in view of later developments, it was a lucky break. Part way en route, Freel drew my attention to the fact that the chariot's locker, which was mounted immediately abaft the No. 2's seat, had disappeared. Whether this had been caused by our interesting launch from *Trooper* or by something else I never found out. However what it meant was that the locker's contents, namely a spare set of oxygen bottles, three or four auxiliary charges we were supposed to affix to the hull of any minor warships we came across, and, more important, the two large magnets with short attached lines by which we could secure our chariot's warhead to the hull of the target ship, had all disappeared with the locker. The prospects for a successful operation were somewhat diminished.

However, the result was not quite as bad as it could have been. After working our way hand over hand up the inner side of the net to the surface, I steered the chariot across the harbour to where our target, the 8500-ton transport *Viminale* was moored alongside a quay. The ship had a huge overhanging stern, with the rudder post coming down vertically into the water. It happened that, before leaving *Trooper*, I had picked up and fastened to my belt a coiled length of rope, about 15 feet, on the general grounds that it might well come in handy. ("Listen, son; wherever you go in the Navy, take a coil of rope.") It certainly did. I lashed the chariot's warhead to the ship's rudder post, on the seaward side so that it wouldn't be seen from the quay, released the warhead from the chariot, and set the detonation time clock to go up in one hour – (or so I thought; in fact I must have set it for two hours). We then proceeded on the chariot (minus warhead) back to the anti-torpedo net at the harbour entrance, where I scuttled the chariot, and we made our way to the end of the mole, discarded our suits, etc., and in due course made our way on foot out of the harbour.

One more important point in our survival. While I was lashing the warhead to the ship's rudder post, my bottles ran out of oxygen, and I had immediately to switch over to breathing the air around me. This meant that I could no longer dive but had to remain on the surface, head above water. It also meant that if I had not lost the magnets, and thus had tried to affix the warhead under the ship, I would almost certainly have run out of oxygen while under water, and probably died. So losing the locker was probably a blessing.

As you know, Greenland and Ferrier from *Thunderbolt* and Freel and I from *Trooper*, were the only two chariots actually to get into the harbour of Palermo on this operation. Greenland made a perfect text-book attack on the cruiser *Ulpio Triano* which sank it. My attack damaged the *Viminale* to an extent that could not be repaired at Palermo, and the ship was eventually sunk by American PT boats, while under tow to the mainland."

TROOPER at Port Said, 1943 — Maritime Photo Library

TROOPER on the Clyde, September 1942

TROOPER's crest

TROOPER: Seamens' Mess   courtesy Gordon Ridsdale

Lt J S Wraith DSO DSC RN   courtesy Richard Wraith

Ldg Seaman Leonard Williams *courtesy Ivor Williams*

L/Tel Len Thompson *courtesy Gordon Ridsdale*

THUNDERBOLT with chariot containers fitted alongside *Titania* at Loch Cairnbawn

Lt Guy Clarabut DSO RN

It. Reg. *PIETRO MICCA*. Sunk by *TROOPER* 29 Jul 43   Collection Achile Rastelli

Lt R P Webb; Lt R E Youngman; Lt L A S Grant; Lt O F Lancaster; Lt J J Dymoke-Byrne; Sub Lt N Campbell

TROOPER's officers on the bridge, Malta, February 1943

Lt L A S Grant DSC RN (as Midshipman, 1939)

ERA Allison Gillies courtesy A W Gillies

Seven 'TROOPERS' at Malta *courtesy Gordon Ridsdale*
Back Row L to R: Bealing Ridsdale Yeoman* Ward*
Front Row L to R: Stobbie* Gair Thompson* Farnell*.   Those marked * were lost with the boat in October 1943.

TROOPER during her trials, Aug-Sep 1943   Glasgow University Archives

Chariot in Loch Cairnbawn

TROOPER with her chariots, probably at Loch Cairnbawn

Miniature of *TROOPER*'s Jolly Roger   made by the wife of L/S Gordon Ridsdale

ERA Peter Forbes   portrait by EA W V Fry

Chariot XIX, Cook and Worthy, had the liner *Galliano* as main target, with three destroyers as secondary. However, soon after they left *Trooper* Cook had become so ill that Worthy had to take over the controls. He landed Cook on a cluster of rocks at the harbour entrance, where Cook opened his visor and was violently sick. Worthy then courageously attempted to carry out the attack alone. However the combination of rough sea and lack of time defeated this heroic effort, so he sank the chariot and swam to shore to find Cook. But Lt Cook was nowhere to be seen and in spite of careful searching by his No 2, he was never found. The presumption is that in his weakened state he was washed off the rocks and because his visor was open, his suit flooded and he drowned. A downcast and weary Worthy then hid his Sladen suit and headed inland.

Greenland and Ferrier from *Thunderbolt*, on Chariot XXII, had been allotted the cruiser *Ulpio Traiano* as main target, with four destroyers for their limpet mines. Theirs was almost a copybook attack. Having attached their warhead to the cruiser and set the timer for two hours, they proceeded to attach mines to the destroyer *Grecale*, the torpedo-boat *Ciclone* and the small mv *Gamma*. Their compass had failed and as a result there was no possibility of returning to *Thunderbolt*, so they scuttled their chariot, sank their suits and went ashore into the unknown.

The second of the chariots from *Thunderbolt*, No XV with Miln and Simpson aboard, met with disaster, perhaps caused by their very rough launch. As they neared the shore, it's battery exploded, flooding the buoyancy compartment. The chariot immediately plummeted towards the sea-bed. Simpson somehow became entangled with the chariot and was unable to free himself. Miln's best efforts to help him were unavailing and at a depth of 95 feet, with the onset of oxygen poisoning apparent, he had to surface in a hurry. He too swam to shore and headed inland.

All six of the Palermo charioteers that made it to shore were picked up by the Italians and imprisoned for the duration of the war. They had the satisfaction of knowing that their mission had achieved something, because they had seen and heard the explosions that tore the stern off the *Viminale* and sank the *Ulpio Traiano*. The limpet mines failed to go off, either because Greenland and Ferrier forgot to arm them –

according to an Italian report – or because Italian divers removed them before they were due to. Lt Dickie Greenland states, "Some doubt exists for the reason. Compton-Hall reported that the Italians had doubts about the 'lead pencil fuse' method for underwater use. What is certain is confirmed by Dove. We *never* had *any* instruction about these things or ever saw them in training."

The cost of Operation 'Principal' had been high. A valuable submarine and her crew were lost – two, if *Traveller* is included, although that is not entirely fair because she was on a patrol and her reconnaissance of Taranto formed only part of her task. Two others were unusable for normal work until their containers were taken off; twelve skilled charioteers were killed or died. There was also the cost of the chariots, the containers and many weeks of training. Against this, a cruiser was destroyed and a troopship severely damaged. In purely monetary terms it was an expensive way to wage war. As Captain (S) Ten, Simpson, said, "…the prolonged use of three T class submarines exclusively for chariot work and the loss of one of them, seems a disproportionate price to have paid." What he does not say, perhaps because he did not know at the time, is that the Axis forces were put to considerable trouble in tightening their security. This was the direct result of a signal from Kesselring and represents one of the unmeasurable benefits that accrued from the attack. What is certainly not in doubt is the dedication of and courage exhibited by the Charioteers in carrying out their task.

Simpson himself, after two years and two weeks in one of the most gruelling commands imaginable, throughout the period of what was effectively a siege of Malta and during which he had to endure the agony of seeing so many of his beloved boats depart but never return, was about to relinquish command of the Tenth Submarine Flotilla. His General Letter No.19, headed HMS *Talbot* and dated 20th January 1943, is addressed to the Flag Officer Submarines, with copies to the Commander in Chief Mediterranean (Admiral Cunningham), The Vice Admiral Malta (Admiral Leatham), Captain (S) One, HMS *Medway II* (Captain Ruck-Keene) and Captain (S) Eight, HMS *Maidstone* (Captain G B H Fawkes). It begins with an apology. He regrets the operational side of his monthly letters has not been kept up because of "the necessity for my constant presence in Malta Headquarters whilst operating all submarines in the Central Mediterranean." One can only begin to imagine the worries and loss of sleep that that understated phrase implies. He goes on: "I much regret that Operation "Torch" has cost us the loss of HM Submarines *Utmost* (Lt J W Coombe), *P48* (Lt M E Faber) and *P222* (Lt Cdr A J Mackenzie) and Operation "Principal," *Traveller* (Lt D St Clair Ford) and *P311* (Lt Cdr R D Cayley). The circumstances of their loss have been reported to you." That is followed by unstinting praise for the "wonderful courage and skill of those who have gone to sea and fought the enemy, and remark with pride on their results" which amounted to half a million tons of shipping sunk and over a quarter of a million tons damaged.

Simpson's brief on arrival in December 1940 had been to cut the enemy's sea communications between Europe and Tripoli. He concludes his final report by saying "It was therefore particularly thrilling to me when Tripoli fell to the Eighth Army before I left Malta. I wish my successor Captain G C Phillips the very best of hunting on European Shores."

What he did not tell Phillips but related later in his book *Periscope View* was "how much I loathed the way [my task] had developed during the past two months on the Palermo-Tunis route.....there was a gnawing anxiety every hour of every day and night over how my men were standing up to the strain of operating within a narrow channel with barely sea room to manoeuvre, ceaseless enemy air patrols overhead and convoys to attack which now contained invariably twice the escorts than there were targets." The loss of four boats in five weeks had clearly greatly upset this brave and caring man, who was by his own account glad to hand over to someone else at last, on 23rd January.

* * *

Trooper was hardly tied up in Malta before her containers 'were removed in dockyard.' Simpson was anxious to have his submarines back doing their normal work of war patrols. However *Thunderbolt* was not relieved of her containers until she had completed Operation 'Welcome.' This was a two-chariot attack to forestall any Axis attempt to sink block-ships at the entrance to Tripoli harbour. She succeeded in getting her chariots launched, in spite of the presence of an E-boat a few hundred yards away, then slipped gratefully away underwater. The attack was partially successful, one of the two block-ships being sunk before it was properly positioned, so that an entrance to the harbour remained open. Of the two chariot crews – the only ones left on Malta after 'Principal' – Lt Larkin and PO Berey on XII had technical problems but managed to reach the beach after sinking their chariot and ditching their gear. They managed to evade capture until the Eighth Army arrived. Sub-Lt H L Stevens, who had not long since taken part in the attack on Palermo, was on XIII with Chief ERA Stanley Buxton. They were less lucky, for although they managed to attack their target successfully, they were captured after going ashore. Theirs was the last wartime operation carried out from a British submarine using containers to carry chariots.[19]

* * *

For her second patrol – albeit her first proper war patrol as a hunting submarine – *Trooper* had a replacement captain in command, as Lieutenant Wraith was in hospital. This was Lt R P Webb, RN, who had been sent to the USA in 1942 to fetch the ex-American S-class boat *S24*, renamed *P555* – but he had relatively little experience of the Mediterranean war. She also had a very young new officer, Sub-Lt The Hon Neil Campbell, RN, who had joined on 28th January and would make six patrols with her. "[The] Port Argostoli area was chosen for the first day's normal war patrol for *Trooper* to settle down."

The Patrol Report states: "TROOPER sailed from Malta on the 3rd February 1943 to patrol in the area of CORFU, LEVKAS and CEPHALONIA." Peter Forbes's diary says:

---

[19] Chariots *were* used again – for beach reconnaissance in advance of Operation 'Husky' (invasion of Sicily) and elsewhere but were carried on the parent boat's casing *without* containers. Also later carried by MGB's.

3rd February.

Left Malta for 14 day patrol. Our Captain is in hospital so we have a temporary Captain to do this one patrol.

4th February.

Our patrol is to be off the coast of Greece to the toe of Italy, supposed to be a quiet billet. This Captain is supposed to be no good, according to the knowalls.

6th February.

On our billet now, plenty of enemy aircraft about. Have to go deep occasionally to avoid them. Captain seems to be very efficient.

The Patrol Report states: "Lieutenant Webb first patrolled off ARGOSTOLI and ZANTE; no targets offered, and on 7th he moved off to cape DUKATO. No worthwhile targets were sighted there, so he moved on the 10th to the vicinity of ANTI-PAXOS. Peter Forbes's account:

7th February.

Plenty of enemy schooners about, small things, too small to waste a torpedo on and too dangerous to go to gun action against them.

9th February.

Sighted a 9,000 ton vessel coming out of an Albanian Port [should be Greek], full speed towards it to get ready to attack, when lo and behold a red cross begins to appear on the ship's side, a hospital ship! What a let down, many of us were of the opinion to sink it (we are a bloodthirsty crew). For all we know, it may be full of troops. Left it to go unmolested on its way.

10th February.

Have been watching a railway bridge on the mainland all day, plenty of long trains have crossed it. May go to gun-action to wreck it, risky job though. Four months married today.

12th February.

Working our way up the coast, nothing of any size yet. Plenty of aircraft about though.

13th February.

Off the island of Corfu, chased three small ships on the surface last night but they escaped us in the darkness and the mist that sprung up. Plenty of enemy aircraft flying around, we expect a convoy to pass us tomorrow. The aircraft will be clearing the way for it. They hope!

The official account, from The Captain (S), First Submarine Flotilla, HMS *Medway II*, was rather sterner: "On the 13th, while still off ANTI-PAXOS, two dark objects were sighted at 2336 in calm sea and bright diffused moonlight. TROOPER dived and the target was just visible through the periscope but soon disappeared. [Lt Webb] surfaced at 0400 on 14th, but unfortunately visibility decreased, and he did not contact them again. It is considered that Lieutenant Webb would have been wiser to have shadowed them on the surface until he had a very fair idea of their course and speed, and then working ahead of them out of sight, diving and waiting for their approach. This has often been tried by more experienced commanding officers with success."

The patrol had not been a complete blank, however, for at 1115 on 14th February, the officer on watch sighted a destroyer coming out of one of the ports, followed shortly after by a merchantman of between 4,000 and 6,000 tons – and they had air cover. From her position three miles off the Greek coast, *Trooper* moved to intercept the merchantman. Webb had decided to try for it first and then if the situation permitted, have a go at the destroyer. There were some moments of suspense as they waited for the enemy vessel to reach the desired point. At 1211, in position 39° 06′ N 30° 29.5 E, with the enemy on a course of 128° and at an estimated speed of 10 knots, Webb aimed at a point two thirds ahead of the merchantman and in line with the destroyer's after mast. The range was 4,300 yards and the torpedoes were set to a spread of 750 feet. The firing interval between each was 9 seconds. "Fire one! ... Fire two! …. Fire three! … Fire four!" One loud explosion was heard, followed by a second a minute later. Their target had turned out to be a naval depot ship, a worthwhile prize, but *Trooper*'s crew had no time to think of that as she fired two more fish at the destroyer, then immediately dived to 150 feet and shut off for depth charging.

On the way down they heard three torpedoes explode on the shore and immediately afterwards they were surrounded by much closer explosions, as depth charges started falling. "It's not a very pleasant feeling either, looking at the ship's side thinking it may bulge in at any moment," remarked Peter Forbes. However Lieutenant Webb managed to edge quietly away from the destroyer, which clearly had not been hit, and none of the 45 depth charges she dropped caused any damage to *Trooper*.

At 1312, the boat was brought to periscope depth. There was wreckage floating about; a large column of smoke was seen towards Preveza, and a distant explosion heard soon afterwards, further confirmation that the supply ship had indeed been sunk. However Webb did not linger, lest the destroyer return with a fresh load of depth charges.

On the 15th *Trooper* was back patrolling off Argostoli (Cephalonia) but no other targets presented themselves. The Asdic rating was put on Captain's Report for sleeping on watch. It is hard to imagine anything more dangerous than a dozy Asdic operator, for he is the ears of the boat and she and her crew depend for their existence upon his skills. The boat was at 60 feet at the time, avoiding the attentions of enemy aircraft… On the 17th they headed back to Malta, arriving on the 18th with their Jolly Roger flying.

Captain (S), First Submarine Flotilla, Captain Phillip Ruck-Keene, noted in the Appendix to the Patrol Report that "Valuable experience was gained in handling *Trooper* without containers being fitted and of patrol conditions, the slight A/S measures leaving the ship's company remarkably cheerful."

Between arriving back at base and the start of their next patrol, the boat was dry docked for a clean and there was minor work to be done on the engines as well. A rather gloomy diary entry by Peter Forbes mentions buying presents for his beloved Molly "which I will keep till I go home. (If I ever do)."

By the 4th of March, *Trooper* was fully ready for sea again and at 1300 left on her third voyage, to patrol the area north of Messina and the approaches to Naples. She proceeded unescorted down the swept channel and at 1430 dived for a trim before continuing on the surface, on the route given through area QKB.20, passing 12' to the north of Pantellaria. The wind was in the north-east, force 4, and she was making 13 knots. "This patrol is our last from Malta and going to last nearly twenty days," noted Peter Forbes, "We are to operate from the straits of Messina between Italy and Sicily. Ten of us submarines are to work as a sort of wolf-pack. We will finish in Algiers. We hope!"

The CO's report submitted at the end of the patrol gives a good indication of what happened during it. On the evening of the 4th, a Wellington bomber was seen overhead at 100 feet and almost at midnight, a searchlight was seen on Pantellaria. Early on the morning of the 5th, the boat was at periscope depth but by mid-day the swell was too great, so she dropped down to 70 feet and came up for 'routines.' Four distant explosions were heard at six-thirty in the evening – some other boat's torpedoes perhaps – and just before eight o'clock, she surfaced north-west of Marittimo and proceeded on passage to her allotted area on a calm sea. An unidentified low-flying aircraft passed overhead about an hour and a half later and at 10 pm a searchlight was sighted on Cape St Vito.

On 6th March, life became more interesting. *Trooper* dived, as was usual, soon after first light, which was at 0535, and came to periscope depth. She was well out in the Tyrrhenian Sea and it was raining heavily. Fifty to 60 single-engined fighter aircraft were spotted flying south at 50 feet at 0730 but nothing further developed from that, unless they were responsible for the distant explosions heard at 1130, which seems unlikely. It was still raining at mid-day, with a south-east breeze. Then at 1310 a signal was received from Captain (S) Eight, ordering them to be in their given position by 1400 if possible. There was continuous air reconnaissance and at 1358 *Trooper* received a report of a southbound convoy, to the north-west of her. By 1445, through the periscope, Lieutenant Wraith could see aircraft circling very low and went down to 60 feet. Three minutes later, there were Asdic transmissions on the starboard bow and he came back to periscope depth for a look. Eight miles away was a convoy of three merchantmen escorted by four destroyers.

"The rain had cleared a bit and although I was 70° on the port bow, I commenced to close at speed to attack if a zigzag to port was carried out. Unfortunately the enemy zigged to starboard and the range was never less than 4½ miles. Rain obscured the enemy completely and at 1535 I broke off the attack." It was unfortunate that *Trooper* was just too far east, because one of the merchant ships was of 7-9000 tons, the other two being about 2-3000 tons, juicy targets, although well defended by the destroyers and at least five aircraft.

About an hour later a signal from S.8 ordered *Trooper* to proceed after dark to another area, which she did surfaced. Shortly after she had dived at 0505 on the 7th, the letter 'B' was heard on an Asdic transmission to the north-west. There was no hydrophone effect [HE] or other explanation ever found for this mysterious transmission. The boat continued her vigil between three and five miles off the Italian shore. Coastal traffic was remarkable only by its absence and only two aircraft were seen all day. The monotony was relieved by watching the trains steaming along the main line, clearly visible onshore, about ten of them an hour heading north or south. At dusk she surfaced and opened up from the coast until she was 25-30 miles off, where Wraith hoped that there might be some ships heading up from Cape Vaticano to the Gulf of Naples. Disappointingly the only vessel to pass was not a legitimate target, being a fully lit hospital ship heading for Messina.

On the 8th, *Trooper* dived south of Iscolelli Point and patrolled four to seven miles off it all day. "Nothing but small fishing smacks sailing around," wrote Peter Forbes, "Have had a look at the shore through the periscope and you can see quite plainly the little villages and many ruins of castles and churches." It was characteristic of Wraith to make time for his crew during a busy, tense and tiring war patrol.

73

Next day they flogged up and down the Italian mainland off Cape Vaticano at periscope depth, seeing no ships and only three aircraft. Then at 1920 a signal came from S.8 ordering them to a position close north of Cape Milazzo, a small peninsula on the north-east Sicilian coast, to intercept an escorted tanker coming from the direction of Messina. By just after 11pm they were there, stopped, trimmed down and listening. It was dark, with heavy rain showers and occasional glimpses of the lights on Capes Rasocolmo and Peloro burning intermittently. By dawn, there had been no sign of any convoy so, as was usual and prudent, *Trooper* dived.

All morning on the 10th they hung about the Cape Milazzo area, seeing 12 bombers flying west along the north coast of Sicily at 0702, but nothing else. "We thought we had missed it," said Peter Forbes, " but at 3pm just as we were having tea, Captain sighted a convoy of three merchant ships and three destroyers." Wraith's report reads:

"1520   Sighted four aircraft circling to the east.

1545   Heard Asdic impulses on bearing of 070°

1550   Sighted smoke bearing 070°. Commenced attack.

At 1615 the visibility improved to the eastward and I saw at least six ships coming towards, but I could not make out what they were.

At 1620 a heavy rain commenced and I could not see anything for the next 25 mins. HE and Asdic impulses from 3 ships, however, were getting louder and I gave the enemy a course of 250°, to allow them to pass between Cape Milazzo and Vulcano Island. The convoy was obviously going very slowly and the Asdic bearing was hardly changing at all, although I was only running in from the north at 2 knots.

At 1645 the rain lifted and I found myself at 5° on the starboard bow of a large trawler. The convoy did not appear to be formed up properly – it was roughly in two lines with a destroyer ahead and one coming up from astern. The starboard column consisted of one small merchant ship and a large one (possibly a tanker) which I never caught sight of properly as she was well astern in the line, and was bow on to me when I at last got this look. The port wing consisted of one medium sized camouflaged merchant ship of 5000 tons and one smaller M/S [merchant ship], which might possibly have been another large trawler. I speeded up to pass ahead of the starboard wing trawler and she passed astern of *Trooper* at about 100 yards range. I now found myself inside the two columns and perfectly placed for an attack on the 5000 ton M/S [She was the 5470 ton tanker *Rosario*] of the port column.

At 1657 four torpedoes were fired on a 100° track at a range of about 1500 yards. Shots were individually aimed and just after I fired the 4th torpedo I saw one of the aircraft fire two red Very lights. There were two explosions 1 min. 12 secs. and 1 min. 25 secs. after firing the first torpedo. A fairly adjacent depth charge attack followed two minutes later which caused the stern glands to leak and a few minor defects aft. A hunt by two Asdic-fitted ships ensued – 37 charges in all being dropped. This hunt was prolonged but not dangerous, as there was only one exit from this rather enclosed part of the area – to the north. I do not think that either ship was in contact with *Trooper* at any time, although they appeared to be getting firm echoes from us most of the time which was slightly disconcerting. They appeared to be carrying out a search of the area, allowing *Trooper* to be doing three knots, which in fact we were.

By 2310 they had searched up our port side – across ahead and down our starboard side and were pinging on a relative bearing of Green 140°.

At 2315 I surfaced to find a very dark night and heavy rain, and set course to the north."

Wraith's idea of the action and subsequent 'fairly adjacent' depth charge attack was described slightly differently by ERA Forbes!

"We attacked one of the merchant ships, firing two torpedoes, they hit the ship and a destroyer came racing towards us and the Captain calmly fired two torpedoes to try and hit her but she dodged them and immediately dropped a shower of depth charges. They were the nearest we have ever had so far and it isn't a pleasant experience at all. At the first one our lucky horse-shoe had fallen off its hook. The noise of the depth charges gradually grew fainter until they ceased about 9pm, five hours after we attacked them. We stayed down until midnight then surfaced to charge our batteries up."

Sub-Lt Neil Campbell, commenting on the increasing competence of Italian anti-submarine skills, noted that "On this patrol the *Trooper* was very well hunted, unusually so." While Captain (S) Eight later remarked, in reference to the hunt made for her, that "*Trooper* was well extricated from a very awkward position."

Next day *Trooper* drew a blank in the region of Cape Bonifati but was ordered back to the Milazzo area by a signal received in the mid-afternoon. On her way back south, she dived at one in the morning because a dark object was seen off Stromboli but as no HE was heard it was probably the small islet of Strombolioccio. They surfaced again and carried on south, passing inside Stromboli, until at 0430 they dived, came to periscope depth and started to patrol north of Milazzo. By 0700, constant air patrols were being maintained over the area, a sure sign that some shipping was in the offing. This was underlined when two anti-submarine trawlers came out from Messina and began to hunt in the area, using Asdic. A third trawler kept stopping to listen. The sea was so calm that the *Trooper*'s fore-casing could clearly be seen through the periscope. That being so, the risk of being spotted by one of the three continuously circling aircraft had to be high, so she was taken deep and retired to the north.

A couple of peeks through the periscope showed the trawlers still quartering the area, now some four or five miles away and it was not until 1900 that the sound of their HE grew faint as they headed back to Messina. *Trooper* continued to the north of Stromboli, where she charged her batteries before yet again returning to Milazzo.

The trawlers had gone, but there were still some aircraft about. At 1500 on 13th March, a destroyer passed about a mile away, doing 18 knots on a zig-zag course for Messina. At 1600, the boat was ordered to a new patrol area, north of 39° 30′ and east of 13° 30′, well out into the Tyrrhenian Sea and she set course northward. As they travelled, they heard, at 1820, the explosion of one torpedo hit to westward, followed by 40 depth charges dropped in ten minutes – then silence. S.8 – Captain Fawkes – was to write in his summary of the patrol "The explosion and depth charges heard ....were, I regret to say, in all probability the occasion of the loss of *Thunderbolt. ... Thunderbolt* is known to have been some 20-40 miles to the westward of *Trooper* at this time."

In fact what had happened was this. At 2210 on 13th March *Thunderbolt* torpedoed the Italian merchant ship *Esterel* two miles north of Capo San Vito. Following the attack, the torpedo boat *Libra* was ordered to seek out the submarine responsible. The *Libra* made contact with the *Thunderbolt* that night and carried out seven depth charge attacks with no result. On 14th March, at approximately 38°15'N, 13°15'E the Italian corvette *Cicogna* obtained a contact and shortly after 0734 a periscope was sighted 2000 yards off the corvette's bow. At 0845 the periscope was again sighted, this time less than 10 feet away. Depth charges were launched at once and the corvette increased its speed and turned for another attack when an explosion lifted the submarine's stern out of the sea at an angle of ninety degrees. The submarine sank through a discharge of air and oil. A further two depth charges were dropped resulting in air bubbles, oil and smoke appearing on the surface where the submarine had sunk. By 0440 that day *Trooper* was patrolling off Cape Polinuro. At 0900 she heard a further 30-odd explosions to the south west, which, in spite of the distance, must have been *Cigona*'s pattern of 24, which finished off *Thunderbolt*. The *Cicogna* remained on station for an hour but no further contact was made. So passed *Trooper*'s noble sister ship and fellow chariot-bearer, her CO Cecil Crouch and all her brave company.

Between 1300 and 1345, while *Trooper* was at 70 feet below a glassy-calm sea, yet more distant explosions were heard, some 90 this time, again to the south-west but apparently only about 15 miles away. There were no other boats nearby, so it seems certain that this time the noise was not submarine-related. She steamed about all that day, seeing nothing but a distant E-boat and surfaced as usual at night in bright moonlight but had to dive for an aircraft just after 11pm. Resurfacing after half-an-hour, she remained undisturbed until daylight when she dived in position 40° 09' N

13° 50′ E and set course for the Gulf of Naples, where there was slight aircraft activity and once a formation of 20 Caproni 311's flying northward but no targets appeared.

When Wraith took *Trooper* up to the surface at 1945 that evening, the boat was some 20′ south of Bocca Grande and 50 minutes later dark shapes to the westward were sighted, proceeding towards Naples. The moon was fortunately obscured by cloud but the night was light and the visibility excellent. Wraith wasted no time in attacking the second and largest of the five vessels he could discern. Only nine minutes after seeing the ships, he had fired four torpedoes from an estimated range of 4 miles, dived and turned away. Two fairly loud explosions followed, indicating a hit, possibly on one of the following vessels rather than the intended target. There was no counter-attack and when Wraith heard the convoy's destroyer escort retiring in the direction of Naples, he retired to the westward before surfacing at 2325 to begin the routine process of charging *Trooper*'s batteries. The night was not over yet, however, for an air reconnaissance report was received at 2335 with details of a southbound convoy and course was altered to intercept. Some minutes later, a flare was seen about 15 or 20 miles to the north.

Just after midnight, a correction to the aircraft report was received and it was clear it referred to the convoy *Trooper* had attacked earlier. Three more flares were spotted away to the north, before the dawn dive was made at 0420. Enemy activity was brisk, with an E-boat passing at 0530, 36 aircraft flying south very low at 0635, and an E-boat patrolling at 0808. At 1413 on March 16th Capri was bearing 057° and a few minutes later another E-boat was noted patrolling. At 1500 14 aircraft were seen flying north and at 1730 three destroyers passed about eight miles away to the north, making 25 knots. After surfacing at 1950 however, the night passed completely uneventfully.

Trooper dived at dawn in position 40°00′ N 14° 22′ E at 0435 and set a course of 000° to cover the Bocca Piccola entrance. Then "10.30am – Action Stations. Sighted 3 merchantmen and 3 destroyers. Full speed attack under water, periscope depth. Fired three fish at a merchantman then Captain calmly fired 3 more fish at a destroyer. We immediately dived deep. Heard two hits off first salvo then one hit off second salvo. The destroyer was a fast moving target. About 20 depth charges were dropped fairly near us, it's an awful experience waiting for the charge to go off, never knowing whether the next one has our name on it. Suddenly they broke off dropping charges. Picking up survivors again! We gradually come sliding up to the surface again, up periscope and see one of the destroyers alongside a sinking merchantman, taking off survivors. So fired a couple of fish at her. She saw the tracks or the torpedo and came racing toward us. A crash dive and the destroyer just missed cutting us in two, out hearts were in our mouths, as her turbines were so close they sounded like a train in a tunnel. Then followed a couple of hours of more bangs than that. But we finally escaped. Thank God!"

This account by Peter Forbes gives a much more human aspect to the attack, even if it differs in some respects from his CO's. In fact conditions had been ideal, a medium sea with white horses to conceal the periscope and torpedo tracks. There were actually four merchantmen in two columns of two and the three destroyers, one ahead of the convoy and one on either quarter were 'pinging' – that is, actively using their Asdic. Wraith fired three torpedoes at the first ship in the starboard column and three more at the one behind it at a range of 5000 yards. He thought he had hit both ships and possibly crippled the starboard destroyer. One of the other two began an intense hunt for *Trooper* and dropped a total of 22 depth charges over a long period 'which prevented me coming up for a look' as he took his boat out to the south at 3 knots. No mention was made of firing at the destroyer picking up survivors.

There were now only three stern torpedoes left aboard *Trooper*. At 2010 on 17th March she was signalled by S.8 to leave patrol the following evening. This she did after a very quiet day, setting course for Algiers through given positions. At 0131 on the 19th she was in a position 65° east of Cape Cabonara, south-east Sardinia, when she dived for a dark object that was probably a TBD [torpedo boat destroyer]. It must have seen them dive, for it hunted them for 90 minutes using her Asdic, though not dropping depth charges. She nearly caught them, for Wraith was about to surface having heard no Asdic impulses or HE for half-an-hour, when she started up her engines. Wisely perhaps, he remained dived and proceeded on passage.

There were no further excitements before *Trooper* made her rendezvous with the mine-sweeping trawler *Ronaldsay* off Algiers at 0645 on 22nd March. By 0900 she was secured alongside the depot ship HMS *Maidstone*. Gus Britton, a signalman on HMS/m *Tribune* at the time, recalled watching her arrival, noticing: "…her elegant appearance. She was looking so good in her dark-blue Mediterranean livery with a new white ensign and her Jolly Roger flying."[20] It had been an action-packed patrol and officers and men alike were ready for a break.

* * *

To add to the record, both official and that of Peter Forbes, about Trooper's 3rd patrol, there is also a media account by a journalist called Julian Greenberg, who was the British United Press correspondent in Alexandria, which appeared in *The Star* for 30th January 1944. As Greenberg wrote, "Lieutenant Wraith tells the story of a patrol early in 1943 when British submarines were struggling to prevent vital war supplies reaching Rommel's Army in North Africa." This account of the patrol is interesting because it shows what was being told to the public – and almost a year after it happened at that – by the serving officer most intimately involved. The account is clearly very guarded – no names of places or even indication about where they might have been – and of course related in layman's language:

"We were making our way to an area in which enemy convoys might be expected. We had to pass though an enemy minefield to get to it. We travelled submerged by day and on the surface at night.

We kept a good look out when we were on the surface because there were low-flying aircraft about and we were leaving a phosphorescent wake behind us. That is one of the chief worries at night – the phosphorescence gives our position away.

It was daylight when we reached the convoy area. Through the periscope I could see the masts and low-flying aircraft of an escorted enemy

---

[20] Recounted in Kemp, P J: *The T-class Submarine* p.19.

convoy. We were just too late. Nothing is more infuriating to a submarine commander than this, because there is nothing he can do about it. A submarine's speed submerged is too slow to give it a chance to catch up with a convoy. It is impossible – or suicidal – to surface.

The luck changed on the third day out. I stood a few miles outside a big enemy port. The officer on watch sounded the alarm. He had seen some enemy ships coming out.

We got ready to attack. Then a sudden rain squall came up and I could not see more than half-a-mile, but we got a fix on the ships through our hydrophones. The rain stopped as suddenly as it had started and I saw we were well placed to attack. There were three merchant ships, two destroyers, two special anti-submarine vessels and aircraft wheeling overhead.

We were so close I could see the depth-charges ready on the stern of the anti-submarine vessels, ready for us. We fired – and dived as soon as the torpedoes were away.

We heard the roar as the torpedoes struck home – and then the first pattern of depth charges burst all about us. I ordered the engines to slow, stopping occasionally to listen. It was uncannily silent except for the thuds of the depth charges, now distant, now close.

Twice I ordered complete silence. No one was to move about because the anti-submarine vessels were overhead . . . enemy ears were straining at their listening apparatus.

They went away after six hours. I waited a bit. Then I ordered surface stations. We broke surface and I stepped out on deck in the crisp air. All quiet. Nothing in sight. I resumed my patrol next day, off another enemy port.

Two days later, I attacked at night on the surface; I saw five or six shapes, loosed off my torpedoes and then dived and made off, running at speed for some minutes and then stopping to listen.

Alarm again. I could hear the hunters. They moved about pretty closely for three hours, and I told the men not to make any noise. Then the hunters went away and we surfaced.

Next day I saw white horses on the sea and knew that the aircraft would have difficulty spotting us and I moved just below the surface to attack another convoy of four merchant ships and three destroyers coming out of the port.

Torpedoes were fired at two of the merchantmen. These torpedoes found their mark – two on the same ship. Again I dived, ran a little way and then froze in silence. But they were confused above. They didn't get very close.

I came up again that night – and then I got a signal calling me back to base."

* * *

Arrival in Algiers must have been a wonderful relief after a hard patrol, for unlike Malta, Algiers was well supplied and not suffering the same pressure from air-raids, though they were by no means unknown. The depot ship there was HMS *Maidstone*, a sister ship of HMS *Forth*, although almost a year older. She had been based at Gibraltar until it was felt safe to move her to Algiers. Both vessels were built by John Brown's yard and were to remain in service until long after the war was over. At 8am on 21st January 1943, Admiral Cunningham, newly promoted to Admiral of the Fleet, had hoisted his flag in *Maidstone*.

Some idea of conditions may be gained from Peter Forbes. On 25th March he was ashore with two of his messmates and they had had a bottle of champagne to celebrate the anniversary of his engagement. There had been a big air raid expected, because a convoy of troopships had recently docked.

"We rowed off [back to the boat] in the middle of the raid, shrapnel and bullets dropping all around in the water but we were full of Dutch courage and we don't care for those b----- Germans. Came on board and had a few minutes of firing the Lewis guns at imaginary planes. The sky was lit up with tracer bullets and searchlights. It was fun. One ship in harbour was sunk and plenty near misses. Next morning oh! My head!"

In more sombre and reflective mood, he notes that

"I had a few walks ashore here and found many beautiful spots, lovely gardens where all kinds of animals and fish were. While we were here three of our class of submarines were due in and never came. They had been following us up in each billet; as we left another one came up and so on. So we are all worried, wondering if our class are too big for the Mediterranean, too easily seen….. But those three boats were all with us at Malta and we used to know each other very well, meeting at the ERA's club ashore and having good times together. It makes you very morbid to think that they will never return. . . . Never mind, if I survive this war I can say I have done my little bit in it."

Neil Campbell also records the tranquillity to be found ashore in Algiers:

"[There were] two families of French Algerians who looked after in particular the submarine flotilla of HMS *Maidstone* in Algiers. Our visits there were very fleeting but I do remember very well what a pleasure it was to go to their villa out at Sidi Farouche."

Viewing from a loftier perspective, in his autobiography, *A Sailor's Odyssey*, Admiral Cunningham wrote that the success of British submarines against Axis shipping had led to increased anti-submarine activity on the part of the enemy and that "…our submarines were working in conditions of extreme hazard in enemy controlled and patrolled waters. During March we had to deplore the loss of the *Tigris*,

Thunderbolt and *Turbulent* with their brave crews, which failed to return from patrol. It is difficult to find words with which to extol the gallantry and self-sacrificing fortitude of the officers and men of our submarines in the face of their heavy losses. Their spirit, alike with their courage, was magnificent." Cdr Linton of *Turbulent*, who had completed 21 patrols and was due to return to Britain at the end of this one, was posthumously awarded the Victoria Cross. Loss of Lt Cdr Crouch, veteran of 15 patrols and also due home leave, was another heavy blow, as was losing the experienced Lt Cdr G R Colvin of *Tigris*. In fact, according to Neil Campbell, "dismay [at these losses] was so great amongst the Staff that they were convinced the T-class boats were unsuitable for Mediterranean operations because they were too large". A conference was called to discuss the matter, the outcome of which was to keep the T-class boats in the Mediterranean, although *Trooper* for one, was given a quiet area for her next patrol, perhaps to boost confidence, though whether of Staff or submariners is a moot point.

* * *

On 5th April, *Trooper* sailed at 1830 hrs for her fourth war patrol. "Before we left, Admiral of Submarines [Rear Admiral Claud Barry] who had flown from London for a conference [see above], came on board and wished us good luck and a safe return; gave us flattering compliments of last patrol too." wrote Peter Forbes and "We have been promised a quiet billet." This was in Zones E, F and H between latitudes 40° 10' N and 38° 42' N, which they reached on the 9th.

It turned out to be very quiet indeed. They had to dive for a destroyer at 2345 that night and it hung about for an hour and a half, using Asdic, but came nowhere near them. On the 10th they dived for two unidentified aircraft but nothing more was seen or heard until they were thirty-eight miles north of the island of Ustica on the 14th, when five destroyers were sighted approaching, again using Asdic. On both occasions it is possible *Trooper* had been seen or detected. However, each time Lieutenant Wraith was able to retire from the scene without being attacked. The same night, an RAF Wellington dropped a flare very close and then circled round, so *Trooper* dived, just in case the Royal Air Force failed to recognise that she was on their side.

On the 18th, 114 explosions were heard in the direction where *Unseen* was patrolling and three days later many distant explosions in the direction of *Splendid's* area. Whoever was attacking Lieutenant M L Crawford's *Unseen* fortunately had no luck and indeed she went on to survive the war. Lieutenant Ian McGeoch's[21] boat was spread along a line with *Sahib* and *Unruffled* on the expected route of a convoy bound for Tunisia. *Splendid* was the northernmost boat of the line and was in a position about four miles south of the island of Capri. He started an attack on a strange-looking destroyer but it spotted him and engaged with depth charges. *Splendid* received a mortal wound and was 'blown' to the surface, where McGeoch gave the order to abandon ship. The destroyer – which was built in 1938 for the Greek navy by Yarrow's of Scotstoun, had been sunk, then salvaged, by the Germans, refitted and renamed *Hermes* – began firing on the surfaced boat, killing 18 of her crew before they realised that they were abandoning her. *Hermes* then rescued five officers and 25 ratings, all of which of course became prisoners of war. McGeoch and his First Lieutenant, Robert Balkwill, had opened the main vents by hand before abandoning, thus ensuring *Splendid* would quickly sink and not fall into the clutches of the enemy. McGeoch's story is related in his autobiographical book *An Affair of Chances.*

A drifting lifeboat was seen through *Trooper's* periscope on 22nd at 1615. It was investigated but found to be empty. There were no further incidents and she arrived back at Algiers on 25th April, tying up alongside *Maidstone* outboard of *Ultor*[22] (Lieutenant George Hunt), after what Captain (S) G B H Fawkes described as "a very disappointing patrol for the Commanding Officer and his company."

* * *

Two of *Trooper's* officers left at this time and one new one joined. On the 27th Lieutenant R E Youngman, RNR, 'left to *Maidstone'* and Lieutenant May joined. Youngman eventually got his own command, the Scotts-built S-class submarine *Spearhead,* on 16th October 1944. With her, on 27th July 1945, he towed the midget

---

[21] McGeoch was born in Helensburgh in 1914, joined the Royal Navy in 1933 and became a submariner in 1937. He retired in 1970 as Vice Admiral Sir Ian McGeoch, KCB, DSO, DSC.
[22] *Ultor* successfully survived the war and was scrapped in 1946.

submarine XE-4 (Lt Max Shean, DSO and bar, RANVR, with divers Sub-Lieutenant K M Briggs DSC RANVR and Sub-Lieutenant Adam Bergius DSC RNVR) into position at the mouth of the Mekong river for Operation 'Sabre,' which was a successful attempt to cut Japanese undersea communications cables. Two days later Lieutenant J J Dymoke-Byrne, RNR, also 'left to *Maidstone,*' from where he went to General Service on 17th May. Both these officers were 'non-volunteer' – in other words, had been posted to submarines. Roy Edmund Youngman was awarded the DSC for his patrols in *Trooper.*

Algiers was a rest but not a holiday, for the war was ever-present, as again notably recorded by Peter Forbes: "29th April 1943. Some more bad news for our flotilla, three more of our submarines have been lost, *Sahib, Regent* and *Splendid.* All pals of ours too. We must be a very lucky boat or our Captain must be the best out here. It is a very morbid mess on our depot ship watching the gear of our old buddies being packed away out of their lockers to go home to be sold as dead men's effects." *Sahib* (Lieutenant T H Bromage) had in fact had her pressure hull holed in a depth charge attack on the 24th and with no possibility of repairing it, she surfaced, where she came under machine gun fire. Only one crew member died and the boat was scuttled in position 38° 30' N, 15° 15' E. *Regent* (Lieutenant Commander H C Browne) was not so fortunate and almost certainly hit a mine near Monopoli on the 18th, being lost with all hands.

The harbour at Algiers was a busy place and on 1st May the battleships *Rodney* and *Nelson,* two cruisers and 20 destroyers put in. The submarines were moved around according to need. On 7th May *Trooper* moved outboard of *Saracen*[23] to store ship. At 0730 *Seraph*[24] secured to her port side. Finally, on the 11th she slipped to sea for Malta at

---

[23] She was depth charged on 7th August by the Italian corvettes *Minerva* and *Euterpe* off Bastia in NE Corsica. The crew abandoned ship and the boat was scuttled.

[24] This boat, under her CO Lieutenant 'Bill' Jewell became famous as 'The Ship With Two Captains' when transporting French General Giraud, who refused to travel on a British ship. *Seraph* was therefore temporarily given an American CO. She was also the boat who 'launched' the body of 'The Man Who Never Was' off the coast of Spain in a successful attempt to deceive the Germans about the location of the invasion that was to take place on Sicily. She had many other adventures and survived until 1963.

1830 after inspection by Captain (S). *Trooper* was leaving the 8th Flotilla and going to join the 1st, based at Beirut.

Their passage to Malta was thankfully uneventful. They had on board a Polish officer and six ratings, plus as much in the way of T-class spare parts as they could squeeze in to every available space. Twenty miles north of Algiers on the 11th they encountered HMS *Eggesworth* [I have been unable to find any other reference to this vessel. DRG]. As signalled by S.10, between the 12th and the 16th they passed through Area QBB.65, having a quiet journey past Pantellaria on the surface on the night of the 13th, seeing on the way 12 Beaufighters flying north-east on the 15th and a solitary Swordfish heading south-east on the 16th. More sinister were the many potentially lethal floating mines observed 30 miles north of Gozo, so it was no doubt with some relief that they made their rendezvous with the minesweeper at the end of the north east swept channel at 0830 on the 17th. At 1115 they arrived at *Talbot* and secured to the port side of *Medusa*. Ten minutes later they were joined by Lieutenant Daniell's *Unison*, which tied up on their starboard side.

This stay in Malta was brief, only five days in fact, though long enough to experience an air raid on the 21st. It and several others that followed were no doubt trying to hit a convoy that had arrived that morning, but unlike in former times, the British fighters were able to drive off the enemy aircraft before they reached the island. One of the enemy was brought down by the combined fire of three of the island's anti-aircraft guns. *Trooper*'s log for 22nd May records that at 0800 hands were preparing the ship for sea. More interestingly, the entry for 1100 reads "six special services (other ranks) joined ship." This 5th patrol clearly was going to involve doing something slightly different.

* * *

Commando operations were being undertaken frequently throughout the eastern Mediterranean at this time, using submarines to land them and, with luck, extract them after they had finished whatever task they had to do. So it cannot have been a surprise for *Trooper* to find herself with a group of them as passengers. The most common delivery system involved the submarine surfacing about a mile offshore of the landing point and for the commandos to paddle in using folbots.

The folbot was derived from one of a number of commercially-produced kayaks that, as the name implies, could be folded up for transport and storage. A German tailor, one Johann Klepper, produced what was almost certainly the first model back in 1910, creating a sectional wooden frame that could be rapidly assembled and inserted into a canvas skin, which formed the hull. Essentially, little more was required to complete a most seaworthy craft, except to tighten the fixtures and insert the seats. The rival Folbot Company began life in London in 1933 but moved to Chicago in 1935 and later to Long Island, where the company recently celebrated its 70th anniversary. Klepper too, still exists and their products are so good as to be the preferred choice of the special forces of several nations. Wartime kayaks were initially built in London by a different group and turned out to be inferior, mainly because of poor-quality materials and indifferent workmanship. However the name folbot persisted. The problems were overcome and the operational folbot, now virtually redesigned by the commandos who used them, was tough enough to become standard transport for clandestine landings by small parties of men.

The chief difficulty arose from the fact that each kayak could only carry two people. With the limited space available in submarines to stow them, even when folded, the time spent putting men ashore – bearing in mind the vulnerability of a surfaced submarine in shallow water – was greater than desirable. One answer to this was to carry an assault craft on the boat's casing. This left it exposed to the risk of being damaged during passage and much effort was put into finding a craft tough enough. Major R J C Courtney, MC, who was the CO of the Special Boat Section, carried out trials with a craft known as the Uffa Fox Pontoon, which could carry 20 men, in conjunction with HMS/m *Ursula*[25] (Lt R B Lakin, DSO). More tests were made on the

---

[25] *Ursula* was launched in 1938, had a very busy war, with several well-known CO's and survived to be scrapped in 1950

Clyde in June 1942, using P614 and P615[26] and men from units of 6 Commando and 12 Commando. Captain (S) Three – Captain H M C Ionides at that time – reported favourably on the outcome, with some reservations about its weight and the effect this could have on handling it on a boat's casing in poor weather.

* * *

When she slipped for sea at 1700 on the 22nd May, *Trooper* had folbots aboard and an assault craft on her casing, as she followed Lt Cdr R H Dewhurst's HMS/m *Rorqual*[27] out along the swept channel. Her patrol area this time was in the Adriatic and off the west coast of Greece, with a scheduled stop offshore from the island of Zante to land her passengers.

They arrived in position on the 25th and at 2110, as soon as it was dark enough, Wraith closed land off the south coast of Zante, to begin what was officially known as Operation 'Entertain.'

"We went within a mile of the island on our motors, stopped, put off two canoes, one empty and being towed by the other canoe containing an officer and a corporal. The object was to land, damage one of the canoes, put stale sandwiches and empty beer bottles in it and leave it there," wrote Peter Forbes. "We think it is to give the enemy a scare and keep them busy when they find it." By 2150 the folbots had been successfully launched and *Trooper* withdrew to safer waters to await their commandos return.

At 2300, *Trooper* closed the land again, located the commandos and by 2355 had them safely back aboard and the remaining folbot restowed.

On the 27th, the boat dived through the Straits of Otranto, a dangerous, narrow and heavily mined channel that took them into the Adriatic. A ship was sighted but they left it alone because attacking it would not only have been foolhardy

---

[26] These two boats were built for Turkey but retained on the outbreak of war. They 'starred' in the film "We Dive at Dawn" with John Mills. P614 was given back to Turkey in 1946 but P615 was sunk on 18th April 1943.

[27] *Rorqual* was one of six Porpoise-class minelayers and the only one to survive the war unscathed.

in the narrows but more seriously could have compromised Operation 'Tiger,' which was their next job. According to Peter Forbes's diary, they were the first British Submarine to enter the Adriatic since January, when it had become too dangerous to operate in. And it was still dangerous. "This afternoon we heard wires [mine cables] scraping along the hull. It is a nerve-racking moment, waiting on the explosion you won't hear. The silence in the boat is deadly, you can cut it with a knife. The Captain managed to get us out of the danger, he is very good. We would follow him anywhere."

Once safely through, they cruised up and down the coast about three miles off from Vieste, until the 30th, looking for a suitable landing spot for the commandos. Vieste lies at the easternmost point of the Promontorio del Gargano, the stubby spur of land that sticks out a bit above the heel of Italy. At 2140 they came close inshore, in water with a depth of just 60 feet, which left little chance of diving to escape should the need arise. "At 9pm we went into a little bay on the surface, to within a mile and a half of shore, opened the hatch and got two canoes out and eight big water-tight tins of explosives and a transmitting and receiving wireless set." The assault craft on the casing had been damaged by rough weather (presumably during times spent on the surface during battery charging) but the shore party managed to embark everything, including themselves, using just folbots. As soon as they were all away, *Trooper* proceeded clear to a safer position and charged her batteries.

At 0215 on the 31st, a successful rendezvous was made with the commandos, using pre-arranged signals, despite it being a velvet-black night. They had succeeded in burying the explosives and wireless set and marking the spot with some coloured rock they had brought from Malta for the purpose. Agents would later collect the equipment for use in sabotage work. There was a nasty moment during re-embarkation when a patrol-boat passed quite close. All machinery was stopped and doubtless about 70 sets of breath held until it departed. It had only to play its searchlight into the bay to have given the shore batteries a sitting target to fire upon....

On 1st June they were patrolling off Bari, dived at dawn and almost immediately went to Action Stations, Wraith having seen a dark shape. As it grew lighter, it resolved itself into a small tanker of about 800 tons escorted by a destroyer. He did not think it was a target worth the risk of attacking, as the torpedo tracks would have been all too clear. "Our Captain is a very sound man, not one of those 'Daily Mirror' Captains who take all sorts of daft risks just to get their name in the papers," commented Peter Forbes to his diary.

Again on the 2nd a large merchant ship was sighted, steering for Bari and later a liner approaching from the south. Both were too far out of range to attack, but from watching them, Wraith was able to judge the seaward end of the swept channel, so he closed with it and waited to see what might appear. They waited around all night and all next morning but it was very hazy and at six miles out they could see very little anyway. Then towards tea-time on the 3rd, a 2-3000 ton merchantman, the *S. Catello*, came steaming out. Action Stations was sounded and an attack immediately commenced. At 1620 a salvo of four torpedoes was fired at 110° and a range of only 1400 yards. And all of them missed. As Captain (S) One, Phillip Ruck-Keene was to state in his report "It is very difficult to explain how those torpedoes missed." Obviously having seen the torpedoes' tracks, the *S. Catello* at once put back in to Bari. Peter Forbes noted what might well have been the explanation. During the attack, *Trooper* kept hitting patches of fresh water. Fresh water has a different density from salt water and this can drastically affect a boat's buoyancy and thus also her trim. Just as the torpedoes were fired, the boat gave a lurch forward. This could have been just sufficient to divert the torpedoes off course, or perhaps aim them too deep. Wraith brought the boat to periscope depth again but the ship was already out of range. The sole blessing was that the escort did not come and depth charge them.

It was time to leave, on the long passage for Beirut. *Trooper* passed safely out of the Otranto Straits. She sent a signal to Malta at 2345 on the 5th, reporting that the commando operations had been completed successfully and pointed her bows sou' sou' east. They passed Crete on the 6th and Peter Forbes commented "This week we have been on very low rations. One gallon of water per day each man, for all purposes. Our food is low. Bread, one loaf between eight of us per day. Glad to get into port to a decent meal." That was expected to be at some time on the 13th.

On the night of the 12th, *Trooper* altered course at 2300 to avoid large floating wreckage but either they had spotted it too late or there was more of it about than was clear in the darkness, for she struck it. Vibration started up at once in her port propeller shaft, clearly indicating damage to the propeller itself. Fortunately they were now only a few hours out, for at 0740 on the 13th the log states "Arrived and secured Beyrouth Harbour [sic]."

The delight of being allowed to bathe before they arrived was not lost on the crew. "We needed it badly," said Peter Forbes, "the first one since we left Malta." Perhaps even better was the first decent meal for a fortnight – but as they were soon to find out, they had arrived in a land of milk and honey, for war shortages had hardly affected Lebanon.

Captain J S Stevens (of *Unruffled*), on leave from Malta, had found Beirut

> "… abounding in fleshpots of all kinds and cosmopolitan glamour. The First Submarine Flotilla had been based there since 1942, when their depot ship *Medway* had been lost by torpedo. Captain Ruck-Keene commanded the Flotilla and base[28]; he had taken vigorous steps to build up good facilities for maintenance, repairs and accommodation as well as rest and relaxation of the submarines' crews. There were a number of requisitioned cars with chauffeurs, a comfortable rest camp in the hills and special arrangements at hotels.
>
> With submarine friends I saw the sights, including the Cedars of Lebanon and the ancient city of Baalbek; we made the rounds of cabarets and night spots in Beirut. I have never found it easy to keep my weight down; under the conditions of the Malta siege rations a few pounds had certainly come off but while at Beirut I succeeded in putting on eight pounds in seven days. Perhaps coming in runner up in an eating contest with six friends at a restaurant contributed to this."

---

[28] Ruck-Keene vividly describes setting up the Beirut base, known as *Medway II*, in a letter to Adm Max Horton in *Max Horton and the Western Approches*, Appendix IX.

A few days after they arrived, *Trooper*'s crew was given their first proper leave since they left Loch Cairnbawn back in November. Once more it is Peter Forbes who sets the scene:

"This is the best submarine base the Navy have, an old army barracks. The very best of everything: pictures every night and an ice-cream bar; plenty of fruit here, the first time we have seen bananas for years. We are working tropical routine to get repairs done to our machinery and expect to be a fortnight in harbour before going to Port Said dry dock to have our spare screw fitted on. I have just spent three days up at Aley, the rest camp for submarine crews. It is a lovely place, 2,000 feet up in the mountains. In the morning you get a clear view down to the sea. At night we are covered with clouds and mist. One day we took a trip by bus to Damascus, the oldest city in the world standing today. The road climbed to a height of 6,300 feet, turning and twisting, then far below us we saw a flat, fertile plain, "The Plains of Lebanon." Then came the journey down. The driver had his gears in all the time, rounding sharp corners, seeing a sheer drop from the road. Not a drive for a weak person. A few army convoys passed us on the way and also a mule train. Then we saw the mountains. Lovely rugged countryside. In the valley the people still used primitive methods on the land, cutting crops with a hand knife and putting it in stacks by hand too. The plough is only a piece of wood with one handle, pulled by a camel or a bullock. We passed an Armenian village with its mud huts with the fire in the centre. The mule is still the means of transport used by the Arabs. We then climbed out of the valley again up tortuous bends to 5,000 feet. Above us we could see snow-capped mountains. They must have been very high as we were sweltering in the heat.

Just before we reached Damascus we passed about ten miles of barren land just like the wilderness mentioned in the Bible. Damascus itself has its two contrasts, the old and the new. The old contains all the mosques and bazaars with the natives beating out silverware by hand. Not having much time we could not go into any of these places. The new architecture is lovely, the city has its different quarters, Jewish, Moslem, Arab, Greek and of course the white colony. The women mostly wear veils over their faces.

The journey back was in the cool of the evening. As we climbed the mountains we met the clouds and mist, this proving very chilly. Arrived back in the rest camp tired and hungry. It had been a very interesting journey.

Those three days rest are the first we have had since we left home and we deserved it as the patrols here are no picnic. Our stay in Beirut was very nice indeed, a nice clean bed to sleep in at night with a mosquito net over us, and plenty of food. The shops are full of unrationed food and clothes but the prices are extortionate, far above our rate of pay."

Aley features in a series of photographs in the possession of Gordon Ridsdale. Captain (S) One (Ruck-Keene) encouraged crews to enjoy their time of rest and as well as tours to places of interest, skiing trips were organised. Gordon also told about a trip into the desert with a jeep by a party of 'Deep Sea' Rover Scouts among the crew. The war however, was still requiring to be waged.

According to her log, *Trooper* had some shuffling about of personnel while at Beirut, before she proceeded to Port Said, under a new skipper because Lt Wraith, who suffered severely from septic boils on his back, had been hospitalised for a week or two.

15.06.43   a.m. Lt Ryder RANVR joined ship from MEDWAY II.[29]

16.06.43   a.m. 1 P.O. discharged to MEDWAY II. 1700 Stbd watch on leave.

18.06.43   a.m. 1 AB (G.L.) discharged sick to MEDWAY.

19.06.43   0700 Moved and turned round, bows S.

21.06.43   Moved and turned round, bows N.

---

[29] The original *Medway,* a purpose built submarine depot ship, was sunk off Alexandria while shifting to Beirut.

23.06.43	a.m. Lt G S C Clarabut assumed command. Lt Wraith sick ashore. 1 L/S (L.R. 2s/m) joined from MEDWAY.
24.06.43	a.m. 1 S [?] dischg'd sick to MEDWAY. p.m. 1 S [?] joined from MEDWAY.
26.06.43	1030 Captain (S)1 and Greek Minister inspected ship.
	2015 slipped for sea.
	2110 exercise gun action with dummy. Passage for <u>Port Said.</u>
27.06.43	1730 ex. attack.
	1750 Gyro failed; log stopped. To 300 ft for 5 minutes.
28.06.43	0750 Picked up pilot.
	0820 sec. port side to jetty <u>Port Said</u>.
	0300 in floating dock.

Peter Forbes noted that it was "very warm with no water around us. The sun hits down on the shell and it is like an oven but the work must be done, so wearing singlet and shorts we sweat drops of blood. No wonder I am growing thin." They were only there for a week, to have their spare propeller fitted in place of the one that had been damaged and other minor maintenance and repairs attended to, but the crew was billeted on land and was given some shore leave.

Peter Forbes again: "3rd July. Had a walk ashore and this place is like all other cities I have seen out here. The native part is terrible, while the fashionable part is very nice. We stayed at an old hotel, "Southways," converted into a barracks. Our view is right on to the main street." Next day Peter collapsed, with a temperature and terrible pains in his stomach, diagnosed as suspected appendicitis and was rushed to hospital.

Aboard *Trooper* meanwhile, work went on. On Saturday 3rd, Sub-Lt W A T Rayner, RNR, joined from *Medway*. By the evening of the 5th, the new prop had been fitted and everything else done that needed to be or could be. On the 6th, flooding of the dock began at 0500 and at 0630 a pilot went on board to guide them out to the degaussing range. By 0900 they were back, secured stern-to alongside the wharf and the pilot disembarked. Peter Forbes, fearful of being left behind, which might have entailed a very long spell at Port Said, left hospital "still shaky" but clearly not suffering appendicitis, and rejoined the boat.

* * *

Lt Clarabut was "suspected to be a wild devil." He certainly exercised the crew hard, as shown both by the log of the passage to Port Said and now the log of the start of patrol No.6, which was destined for the Adriatic and the West Coast of Greece.

07.07.43 0745 Hands employed preparing ship for sea, working torpedoes, storing, etc.

1900 Cdr (S) inspection.

1915 Harbour stations, embarked pilot.

1930 slipped for sea.

2235 dived for trim.

08.07.43 1715 ex. gun action fired U.W.G.'s.

1723-1800 target practice with practice shells at yellow smoke target. Fired machine guns.

1800 resume co. + sp.

09.07.43 0530 Star sights.

0911 dived to 300 ft for test and exercise.

1020 fired U.W.G.

1028 exercised gun action. Resumed previous co & sp.

1830 Dived for a/c.

1856 Surfaced.

2130 Obtained star sights. Ceased zig zag. Co 317°.

Probably Clarabut was simply ensuring that he knew how the crew, who were strangers to him, performed, which was only sensible given that they could be in action at any time. As it was, *Trooper* was able to proceed towards her patrol area on the surface for two days, because the Allies by this time had total domination of the south-east corner of the Mediterranean. By early afternoon on the 11th – which was the first day of the invasion of Sicily – she was in sight of her old stamping ground, off Zante. From the log again:

12.07.43 0600 HE bearing R50.

0605 sighted 1 fishing vessel co. 190°, also 1 A/S vessel, 1 old destroyer, to northward.

0610 diving stations.

0615 Sighted masts to NE.

0645 vessels beyond range. Abandoned attack; patrolled off LEVKAS.

If that was slightly disappointing, Wednesday 14th, off Cape Dukato, on the Albanian coast, was to be less so and filled with pre-breakfast action:

0300 Decr. 275 revs.

0400 Stopped to carry out listening sweep.

0420 275 revs.

0455 Dived. D.R. 254° C.

Pali 6'.0. Co. as req. for patrolling area 3-5 miles off C.Pali.

0600 A few small vessels and one A/c sighted.

0831 Fired 3 torpedoes at 3,000 ton MV [merchant vessel], unescorted, in ballast. MV a/c and avoided.

0837 Surfaced for gun action. Fired 8 rounds, one hit. MV went aground NE Lales Bay.

0841 Dived.

0845 C. Rodoni 032° C. Pali 151° S/Co. 300°

Peter Forbes's account is rather more dramatic:

"We fired three torpedoes, all missed so the Captain decides to go to Gun Action to sink or damage it. Surfaced and got three rounds fired on us. We fired ten rounds, getting a few hits on the merchantman then a shell flew through our casing. All this time two other ships had come on the scene and they too were letting fly at us. This proved too much for us so we have to dive out of the way. We kept at periscope depth and the last the Captain saw of the merchantman was that it had gone on some rocks and was burning fiercely aft. The action had only lasted a few moments by the clock but it seemed ages, all the time expecting a shell to come tearing through the control room. We certainly had a lively reception. A few moments after that a 600 ton schooner came on the scene. The Captain was going to have a go at that with the gun but, when he asked the other Officers' opinion they disagreed so we crept off to a safe area in case destroyers come looking for us. This Captain certainly is mad, taking stupid risks, we will be lucky to get back to port if he carries on this way. Hope we get our own Captain back when we reach port again. If we do!"

For good measure, Captain (S) One's report differs from both these accounts:

"On 12th July [*Trooper*] was off Cape Dukato. After a day here she set off for the Brindisi-Durazzo route. On 14th a 2,000 ton merchant vessel, north of Durazzo, was attacked with three torpedoes, but was missed. Lieutenant Clarabut immediately surfaced and attacked it with the gun. The merchant vessel was hit more than once, which apparently knocked out the after gun and started a brisk fire aft. Before he could completely destroy her, he was forced to dive by aircraft."

This was not the only occasion that differences between the patrol report, the log and Peter Forbes's diary have been noticed. Not everything that happened was always recorded in the ship's log – although minutiae referring to course changes, sea-state and weather were usually carefully noted. It is difficult to know exactly how much any crewman could know about any particular action; however, if their duties were in the control room, they would not only know what the boat was doing but would hear what was being said between Captain, officers and crew. It is less easy to explain discrepancies between the log and the patrol report, except to remember that it was wartime, much was happening and Captains (S) were under a lot of pressure. In terms of *Trooper*'s story, or indeed that of any submarine, it is plain that the broad details usually agree, which is really all that matters.

On the 15th, a signal was received from Captain (S) Ten – who was still in overall command of operations – for *Trooper* to move her billet to the Gulf of Taranto. All morning she patrolled between Cavtal and Molmat, then:

1315 sighted 1000 ton MV in ballast; prepared to gun it.
1335 put deep by Cant Z506 seaplane patrolling at 30 ft.
2006 surfaced.

The Forbes version reads: "Went to gun action stations when we saw a 1,000 ton patrol vessel of some sort. Captain had a look and remarked 'It has only one gun aft.' We got closer and he said 'Oh! It's got one forward also and two amidships.' We all had a groan, expecting a hot reception gunning this ship. An Italian bomber came on the scene then, it flew right low over just as the Captain was looking through the periscope. The water was flat calm and our whole outline is visible at 60 feet deep. We flooded our quick-diving tank to get us out of the way of the expected bombs. Then the explosions came. Near, but we were well on our way to normal routine."

On the 17th, they passed through the Straits of Otranto to patrol, in a line with three other submarines, across the Gulf of Taranto. This was to try and stop shipping leaving for, or returning from, Sicily, where the invasion was proceeding apace. *Trooper*'s position was at the eastern end of the line, in the vicinity of Capo Sta Maria. They had blank days on the 18th and 19th, then early on the 20th they pursued a dark object on the surface. It was zigzagging wildly and they were preparing torpedoes to fire when they had to break off the chase because a destroyer appeared. It made contact and depth charged them for an hour without coming at all near.

At 0300 on the 22nd, a ship was spotted directly astern. It kept following, then when the moon came up it was seen to be an enemy submarine. *Trooper* hastily dived and shortly afterwards her Asdic operator heard a torpedo whizzing by above them. They heard it, and three more, explode at the end of their runs in the distance. *Trooper* prepared to retaliate but she came to periscope depth just in time to see the other boat slide below the surface, barely a mile away. Peter Forbes's place of duty was on the panel in the control room that day and he and the Officer of the Watch kept a constant look-out, lest she surface again, but without result. It was just as well, because this 'U-boat' was HMS/m *Tactician*![30] Captain (S) One remarked later in his report that in view of the closeness of their billets, they should have been ordered not to attack submarines.

A few days later, on the 29th, having received her recall signal, *Trooper* was about to leave for Beirut. Her log for that day was even more sparing than usual:

0300   Broke charge. Proceeded on MM. Set listening watch.

0535   Dived. 230°. Sta Maria Lt. 7'0

0656   Sunk U-boat in posn. 212° Sta Maria Lt 5'½

0730   Santa Maria Lt bg. 023° 6'½. S/co 160°. P.D.

There is no further entry until 2200, when a course alteration is noted. Yet they had just accomplished a feat that was rare – they had sunk an enemy submarine. It was in fact the It Reg *Pietro Micca*, of the Micca class. What had happened was that Clarabut had noticed the Santa Maria light had been switched on and had turned to investigate why. At 0646 a large U-boat appeared on the surface and he carried out an attack at long range with six torpedoes, hitting and sinking her. A small boat was seen putting out to pick up survivors, so without further ado *Trooper* dived and left the scene.

For once there is no entry in Peter Forbes's diary. The patrol ended without further incident and *Trooper* arrived back safely in Beirut on 2nd August 1943. Peter

---

[30] *Tactician* was later deployed to the Far East, survived the war and was not scrapped until 1963.

Forbes was discharged sick and as a result played no further part in *Trooper*'s story, which, as it turned out, was very fortunate for him.

* * *

The sinking of the *Pietro Micca* resulted in Captain (S) making recommendations for awards as follows:

Submitted,

The attached recommendations for decorations for the sinking of an Italian U-boat of the MARCELLO CLASS on 29th July 1943 in position 39° 01' N 18° 57' E are submitted herewith for consideration.

2. A small vessel in the vicinity was observed to lower a boat and pick up survivors, so there can be no doubt that the U-boat was sunk.

(signed) P. Ruck Keene

<u>FOR DECORATION</u>

1. Lieutenant G S C Clarabut, RN

2. Lieutenant L A S Grant, RN

1. Ldg. Stoker RN Robinson   P/KX.88052

2. Ldg Seaman B T Rushton   P/J.114584

3. E.A. 3rd Class W V Fry   P/MX.49222

* * *

For *Trooper*'s seventh war patrol, she was back in the hands of her own Captain, Lt J S Wraith. She departed from Beirut on 20th August for the Aegean, where her first billet was on the Rhodes-Piraeus traffic route. That proved to be devoid of targets, so she was ordered to the north of the Doro Channel on the 25th.

On passage to this new station, she sighted a convoy that included a 4-5,000 merchant ship – but it was abaft her beam and she could not get into an attacking position in time. This was especially infuriating, as the convoy appeared to be heading directly for the area *Trooper* had just quitted.

The Doro Channel was reached on the 27th and the first two days there were also blank. On the 29th an escorted petrol or water carrying vessel was sighted but was not attacked because intelligence had indicated a convoy was expected later. But it never materialised...

A further shift of billet was made during the evening of the 30th, to the vicinity of Samos. Next day, *Trooper* surfaced and bombarded the tanneries at Karlovasi most satisfactorily from a range of 3,000 yards for four minutes. Uncomfortably accurate return fire from shore batteries then forced her to dive before she had destroyed some caïques that were in the harbour, as she had intended to do.

The patrol was then moved yet again, to the Gulf of Salonika, with a day spent off Skyros on her way there. She inspected the harbours of Kupho and Damura on the 3rd of September but without finding anything worth attacking. She then received a recall signal but it was cancelled fairly shortly afterwards and she was ordered to the Skiathos Channel. Here at last was a target, albeit not a very exciting one. A tug was towing a schooner of about 250 tons through the channel and at 1816 *Trooper* surfaced and engaged with the gun. She sank the schooner and left the tug abandoned and ablaze, then picked up two very willing prisoners and set off back to Beirut.

It had been a disappointing and frustrating patrol, with no torpedo targets, although the gun actions had been successful. "We saw considerable numbers of caïques packed with German troops moving across to the islands," Neil Campbell recorded, "particularly the areas north of Kos and Leros, escorted by a few MTB's and ML's [Motor Torpedo Boats and Motor Launches] and a lot of aircraft. The caïques were not really torpedo targets, they were gun targets, being very light in the water, as were the escorts. But with that number of aeroplanes there was no hope of doing anything about it, so we just sat and watched them go." Captain (S) One, now Captain H M C Ionides, who had replaced Ruck-Keene, remarked in his report that when an insufficient number of submarines were available, it was all too easy to fall between two stools when attempting to order interception.

* * *

Before continuing *Trooper*'s tale, it is necessary to take a look at the war situation in the Eastern Mediterranean as it was in the latter half of 1943.

On the 8th of September 1943, the Italians capitulated. As a result of this, among many other changes, the British were able to take over the Dodecanese Islands. This however did not suit Germany. The Luftwaffe already occupied two good airfields on Rhodes. The Italians had failed to resist the Germans and 35-40,000 of them had been taken prisoner on 11th September. Rhodes was only 70 miles from Kos – and the Germans had two more airfields on Crete as well. In addition they had bomber bases at Larisa and Salonika on the Greek mainland, with dive-bombers at Megara and Argos, also on the mainland. By contrast, the Royal Air Force had a very vulnerable fighter field on Kos but their main airfields on Cyprus and at Gambut in Libya were too far away for fighters to cover the Dodecanese from.

British troops from the Middle East had moved into the islands of Kos, Leros and Samos and other islands in the Dodecanese immediately after the Italian surrender. It was thought that with Italian co-operation they could maintain themselves until such time as it was possible to launch an attack on Rhodes. On 10th September a pre-emptive British-Greek mission had gone to Samos. Our swift intervention also prevented the enemy from carrying out their intention to walk unopposed into Leros and Kos. However by the 19th the Axis forces, that is Germans and pro-Nazi Italians, had occupied Thasos, Samothraki, Limnos, Lesbos, Chios, islands in the Sporades and Cyclades, Kasos, Karpathos, Kythira and Antikythira – as well as Crete and Rhodes. Hitler had ordered that all resisting Italian officers should be shot and other ranks transported to the east to be dealt with as seen fit, so there was great pressure on them. Those that resisted on Kephallonia, where over 12,000 were killed or died on troop transports that struck mines, were the worst example of the massacre of pro-Badoglio Italians but there were others, including, later, on Kos.

Beefing up our forces on Kos, Leros and Samos, especially, was going ahead as rapidly as possible. By mid-September the enemy, realising that something had to be done about this, unleashed their air force. The British intention to use Kos to provide air cover for our ships was theoretically fine – but the Germans were well aware of the threat this posed and began bombing the two airfields. Gallantly though the Allied fighter pilots resisted, they were simply outnumbered and worn down by attrition until by 2nd October only a handful of operational Spitfires were left.

At 0500 on 3rd October, the Germans began Operation 'Eisbär'. After 24 hours the British were in full retreat and by the 6th the Germans were mopping up the last pockets of resistance. *Generalleutnant* Müller, who commanded the invasion, reported "Day passed quietly. Number of prisoners has increased to 886 English [sic] including 46 officers, 3000 Italians. 89 Italian officers shot." Müller was executed by the Greeks in 1947 for war crimes – but this operation had been a brilliant success.

Critically, the Allies were now without effective air cover to protect either naval or land operations in the Dodecanese. Nevertheless, the decision was taken on 12th October to hold Leros and Samos as long as supplies to these islands could be maintained. Four Italian submarines and HMS/ms *Severn*[31] and *Rorqual* were to be used as supply boats, as well as surface craft. Overall policy was to prevent the enemy landing troops, supplies and reinforcements in the Dodecanese. All the while Leros was coming under heavy air attack. To this end, the boats of the First Submarine Flotilla were deployed as follows:

> September, concentrating mainly on the Rhodes traffic
> October, for the first three weeks, close defence of Leros.
> Late October, preventing German reinforcement of Kos and Kalimnos
> November, defence of Leros and Samos.

---

[31] *Severn* had a long career from 1935, that included sinking an Italian submarine and ferrying howitzers to Leros on her casing. She was scrapped in Bombay in 1946.

Several submarines were engaged in this work. *Unsparing*[32] was off the south coast of Kos on 2nd October, to intercept invading German forces and on the 9th was south of Amorgos in the Cyclades, where she sank a 1200-ton troopship. *Surf*[33] was in the Dodecanese, in the Kaso Straits, where she failed to gun a caïque on the 14th of October. On the 16th she towed the *Hedgehog*, 'mother ship' of the Levant Schooner Flotilla, to Levithia and later that day attacked a 5000-ton merchant vessel but had to break off. On the 7th October, *Unruly*[34] was in the Cyclades, where she shot up a merchant vessel, some LTC's and an armed trawler before heading to the south of Amorgos, in the Dodecanese, where she sank a German minelayer. *Unrivalled*[35] was also in the area of the Cyclades, while *Torbay*[36] was in the Dodecanese. And of course *Trooper* was there too.

* * *

On 26th September, *Trooper* had sailed from Beirut to patrol west of the Dodecanese. On the 2nd/3rd October she and *Unsparing* were ordered "to proceed with the utmost despatch to operate off the coast of Kos to prevent enemy ships landing troops." On 10th October she was ordered to a new billet east of Leros. Also operating there were some of the vessels belonging to the Levant Schooner Flotilla, which operated between 1942 and 1945, and consisted of raiding caïques on undercover operations in the Greek Islands, the history of which is a fascinating story in itself. The following account is from Captain S Beckinsale, Officer Commanding HMS *Constantinos* – a caïque in the service of the LSF:

> 14 Oct. 0300   Left anchorage and set course for Leros with permanent action stations as did not know what to expect.

---

[32] Built by Vickers at Barrow, she had a successful career in the Mediterranean. Scrapped in 1946
[33] Built by Cammel Laird. Survived the war and was scrapped in 1949.
[34] Built at Barrow, sank Italian submarine *Accacio* during Op. Husky, (invasion of Sicily). Scrapped 1946.
[35] Another Vickers boat, she also survived the war, to be scrapped in 1946.
[36] Built by HMDY Chatham, she had great success under CO Toby Miers VC, including sinking two Italian submarines. Later sent to the Far East and finally scrapped in 1945.

0700.　　At first light saw a submarine which fired tracer across bows, stopped and all guns ready as it may have been a British or German. Then recognise it as Torbay class. Coming up on submarine's other quarter a sinister form appears and submarine immediately leaves us and goes to intercept, we proceed into harbour. Just as we reach the boom [at Alinda Bay] the aforesaid sinister form comes up and turns out to be Lt Cdr Adrian Seligman in a schooner with its masts lowered. We go alongside *Hedgehog* with Seligman's craft.

This account only makes full sense when coupled with that of Seligman – who incidentally was the founder of the LSF:

"Only once, returning from Naxos in LS8, had I been an actual target – and then it had been in error. It was on a calm night with a brilliant moon. We were lying throttled back off Alinda Bay, Leros, waiting for sunrise before venturing within range of the nervy Italian gunners. Suddenly a submarine surfaced less than 200 yards away to starboard, and next moment tracer from a heavy machine-gun came streaming across our bows. I rammed the tiller hard over, turning towards it, and dived down into the cabin for my uniform cap and jacket. Then a loud and raucous voice, which I remembered well from lively evenings in the wardroom of the submarine base on Manoel island, Malta, boomed out over the loud-hailer 'What ship?' My relief was so overpowering that I let go with the most violent string of expletives I'd ever been sufficiently inspired to put together: 'What the blank, blank, blank and blanking blank are you playing at, Johnny Wraith? This is Levant Schooner LS8. (Exchanging recognition signals would, I believe, have been less convincing.) Then HMS *Trooper* dived. And that was the last I ever saw or heard of Johnny Wraith. "

* * *

Anxiety about *Trooper* was mounting back at the headquarters of the First Submarine Flotilla in Beirut. She was not replying to signals. The hope that the cause was simply equipment failure remained but as her time for return drew closer and was then passed it was evident that she had met with disaster. On the 18th of October, Captain (S) One had to send yet another in the long, sad line of signals reporting the loss of a submarine, that of *Trooper*, "with her outstanding captain and experienced company":

NC"AA"   M O S T   S E C R E T
                18th October 1943

TO: C IN C LEVANT   FROM: S.ONE.

                I M P O R T A N T
       To be decyphered by an Officer specially detailed.

          As TROOPER has failed to answer two signals and is now
24 hours overdue much regret to report she is considered lost.

          In absence of any report or claim by the enemy it is
thought probable cause mines.

          Consider possible but improbable that books are comprom

                                   T.O.O. 18 1120c October
                                   T.O.R. 18 1332c
                                   T.O.R. 18 1529c
SEC: C.O.S. S.O.P. S.O.O. S.O.N.P. D.C. X2 D.A. C.O.S(A)

Jürgen Rohwer, in *Allied Submarine Attacks of World War Two,* lists a torpedo attack that sank the 750 ton German steamer *Marguerite* on 13th October, though 350 of her 900 passengers were rescued and another, unsuccessful, gun attack on the afternoon of the 14th on an Auxiliary Patrol Vessel, as both possibly made by *Trooper.* However, though it would be nice to think that she had added a final few tons to her score before the end, the positions given for the attacks make this impossible. The first was at 38°05′ N 21°02′ E, somewhere in the Ionian Isles and the second in the Kasos Passage, a hundred-odd mile south-west of Leros. Rohwer also mentions the *Bulgaria* and the *Drache,* German mine-laying cruisers that he states were responsible for laying the minefield in which *Trooper* was sunk on the 15th and three destroyers were hit.

```
T/X4                    MOST SECRET CYPHER
                        20th October 1943.

TO  ADMIRALTY (R) FOS  S ONE          FROM  C IN C LEVANT.
    C IN C MED.

Regret to report TROOPER overdue since October 17th
has failed to answer signals and must be considered lost.

    2.    TROOPER was patrolling west of DODECANESE and
for latter part of patrol east of Leros to intercept
expected seaborne attack on island.

    3.    In absence of any other evidence consider probable
cause mines.

    4.    Compromise of books unlikely.

                              TOO 20 0132C October.
                                      (16)

OPL(H)
YCB
```

Thus ended one more submarine story, of too many, that was gallant *Trooper's* tale.

Fifty-three T-class submarines were built and fifteen of them were sunk during the war. *Trooper* was the last of these and the third last boat to be lost in the Mediterranean.

The recommendations for awards that had been made by Captain (S) One on 4th August, after the sinking of the *Pietro Micca* on the sixth patrol, finally came through. Lt Clarabut was awarded the DSO, Lt Grant the DSC, Ldg Stoker Robinson, Ldg Seaman Ruston and EA Fry all got the DSM. They were published in the London Gazette Supplement on 19th October 1943, just two days after *Trooper* had been due back in Beirut. They were the second round of awards made to *Trooper's* men. In the first, Lt Roy Youngman was awarded the DSC, a bar to his DSM was given to A/CPO Watson and ERA Fenn and PO Sleep were both awarded DSM's. Lt Wraith – who already held a DSO from his time on *Upright* and a DSC from even earlier, on *Cachalot* – Ldg Seaman Ruston, Stoker Mott and Able Seaman Whittle were all Mentioned in

Despatches. (For the sake of completeness, it should be noted that Lt Lancaster, who also held the DSC, had been awarded it while serving on *Salmon* in 1939.)

Here is a copy of the notification sent to Lieutenant L A S Grant:

H. & A.925/43.

Sir,

    I am commanded by My Lords Commissioners of the Admiralty to inform you that they have learned with great pleasure that, on the advice of the First Lord, the King has been graciously pleased to award you the Distinguished Service Cross for outstanding bravery, zeal and skill while serving as Navigator in H.M.S. TROOPER in a successful attack on a Submarine of the Marcello class in the Mediterranean in July, 1943.

    This award was published in the London Gazette Supplement of 19th October, 1943.

        I am, Sir,
        Your obedient Servant,

            Sd. R. GLEADOWE

Lieutenant Leslie Alexander Stuart Grant, D.S.C.,
            Royal Navy.

H.M.S. Medway II.

Date ...4th August, 1943.

Recommendation for Decoration or Mention in Despatches.
(M.S.C.M. 81)

Full Christian and Surnames   Leslie Alexander Stuart GRANT (London W.2.)

Rank or Rating   Lieutenant   R.N. Official No. and Port Division

Ship   H.M.S. Trooper.

Whether in possession of any decoration   If so, state particulars

No

Whether previously recommended   If so, give particulars quoting references

No

Whether recommended for   Award of Decoration
or
Mention in Despatches

Nature of Recommendation, whether IMMEDIATE. OPERATIONAL or PERIODIC

Reference to Letter of Proceedings or Operational Report (if Immediate or Operational)

Captain (S) One's letter 06530/424/43 of 4th August, 1943.

Delete as necessary

Description of the services in respect of which recommendation is made

For great zeal and devotion to duty as Navigator during six Mediterranean War Patrols, in the last of which, one Italian U-boat was sunk and a Merchant ship damaged by gunfire. On the last occasion, this officer navigated in shoal water and under gunfire and most difficult conditions and his coolness in a large measure was responsible for the submarine withdrawing without major damage. Throughout, this officer has been a model of efficiency and keenness to all in the submarine, both in harbour and at sea.

Signature

Lieutenant *Rank*

By way of a postscript, I include the following extract from the journal of Sub-Lt Neil Campbell, who had missed sailing with *Trooper* on 26th September because he had a badly septic foot. His comments regarding the patrol, perhaps engendered by his being greatly upset by the outcome, are acerbic:

We had already done one patrol in the Aegean which was pretty futile. ... So this second patrol was crazy. She was sent into shallow waters between Leros and the Turkish mainland, an area most unsuitable for submarines. I had been posted to the operations room while unfit, (they had to keep me employed while the *Trooper* was away), and I expressed to the officer in charge of operations and also to the Captain of the flotilla my astonishment at the choice of area into which *Trooper* was being sent. I didn't see what good she would do there and I thought it unnecessarily dangerous. *Trooper* is reputed to have hit a mine and I remember the ghastly days of waiting in the operations room when she would not reply to any signals. She was lost with all hands. I believe that C in C Levant was responsible for all naval forces operating in the Aegean, not the Captain of the 1st Flotilla. I should mention that *Simoom* was sunk by a mine a few weeks later and the *Seraph* heard a mine mooring wire drag down her side. I was absolutely livid and frightfully upset. To sum up this tragic episode I am very happy to say that I have been in contact with Guy Clarabut who was the spare CO in *Medway* [and as it happened, senior British submarine officer, Haifa, at the time] and Michael St John who was SOO (Staff Operational Officer) for the 1st Flotilla at the time of the submarine operations in the Aegean. St John has confirmed to me that he and Captain S.1 were both equally distressed at the orders received from C in C Levant. He mentioned to me that *Rorqual* also had a narrow escape, in addition to *Seraph*. ...

Guy Clarabut confirmed to me that he was sent with copies of the [charts of] enemy minefields, including the one into which the *Trooper* was sent, to C in C Levant. It would appear that a major submarine disaster was narrowly averted."

The clearly implied criticism Campbell makes of C in C Levant is something I am not qualified to comment upon. Probably no-one is now, at this distance from events. Admiral Sir Henry Harwood, who had held the job, had been compelled to retire on health grounds in March 1943. His place was taken temporarily by Vice-

Admiral Sir Ralph Leatham, who had not long previously been relieved as Acting Governor of Malta, until the appointment of Sir John H D Cunningham to the post. On October 5th, Admiral Sir Andrew B Cunningham was appointed to be First Sea Lord and his place as C in C Mediterranean was about to be taken by his unrelated namesake, Admiral Sir John Cunningham. Admiral Sir Andrew Cunningham describes how, at a meeting they held on 6th or 7th October, "The matter which bulked largely in our minds was the question of the islands in the Dodecanese." There is no doubt that the situation did indeed bulk large in the minds of those at the top. However it is perhaps not unjust to suggest that possibly the details of submarine deployments might have received less than the attention they deserved, because of the changeover in command that was taking place during this critical period in the Dodecanese.

* * *

One final matter requires inclusion:

The German Q-ship GA45 claimed that she had sunk *Trooper*. However, she was in the wrong place, being off Kos, although she was in action there against a British submarine. What almost certainly happened was this: HMS/m *Torbay* was patrolling in the Dodecanese and on 15th October sank a 50-ton caïque by gunfire south of Kalimnos. Later that day, 2½ miles south of Calolino, she sighted three LCT's and a schooner. The schooner was GA45, which counter-attacked, first using depth charges and later, when *Torbay* surfaced, shelling her. *Torbay* dived again and moved away. Clearly GA45 thought that the diving submarine, which was seen going down stern-first, was mortally hit, which was not the case. GA45 was herself sunk on 7th November by the destroyers HMS *Jervis* and HMS *Penn*. I have mentioned this in the interests of accuracy, because a claim that GA45 sank *Trooper* appears in several places in the literature and on the Internet and is undoubtedly erroneous. Moreover, German records contain no information to substantiate the claim.

About GA45 herself, I have established that she was the Greek *Eleni S* (sometimes given as Elleni) and also referred to as UJ2145. I have not been able to find a picture of her, so her appearance may have been that of a schooner, a large caïque or perhaps some small coasting vessel of about 150 tons. "The boat belonged to the Kuestenschutzflottille Piraeus; GA is the abbreviation of Griechenland Aegaeis. This flotilla consisted of a variety of vessels of different types, measurements and armaments. The weak German naval forces in the Eastern Mediterranean Sea had to take any bathtub they could man and armour to establish communication between the isles and render a more or less symbolic protection for transport vessels." As a Q-ship, GA45 would certainly have been well-armed, probably with a concealed 8.8 cm gun, as well as her depth-charges.

HMS *TROOPER*

17th October 1943

J.S. Wraith, DSO, DSC, Captain, Lieut.

L.A.S. Grant, DSC	Lieut.	W.V. Fry, DSM	EA
O.F. Lancaster, DSC	Lieut.	W.C.E. Fenn, DSM	CERA
A.W. Anderson	Sub-lieut.	J. Cornelius	ERA
H.G. Sumner	Sub-lieut. RNVR	M. Peters	ERA
J. S. Ryder	Sub-lieut. RANVR	E. Stott	ERA
J.A. Watson, DSM*	A/CPO	J. Mather	ERA
J.B. Gilbert	PO	M. Forster	ERA
R.B. Sleep, DSM	PO	J.B. Whiting	SPO
B.T. Ruston, DSM	L/Sea	I.D. Bengough	SPO
R.A. Yeoman	L/Sea	P.M. Adam	SPO
L. Williams	L/Sea	R.N. Robinson, DSM	L/Sto
W.B. Whittle	AB	A.F. Legg	L/Sto
F. Smethurst	AB	T.M. Carling	AB
R.S. Chivers	AB	S. Fleming	AB
D. Walker	AB	J.B. Farnell	AB
R. Jones	AB	F.A. Ward	AB
G.W. Hind	AB	E.C. Furnell	AB
S.E. Ribbans	PO/Tel	E. Whatley	AB
L. Thompson	L/Tel	C.C. Lawson	L/Sto
J. Stobbie	Tel	A.H. Mott	L/Sto
F. Crossland	Tel	R.W. Mills	L/Sto
H.C. Cope	Sig	H.G. Horton	L/Sto
H. Skinner	L/Cook	T. Curry	L/Sto
C.J. Stillwell	L/Cook	G. Davies	Sto
F. Charnock	L/Sea	G. Seedon	Sto
F.W. Tripp	AB	A. Brotherston	Sto
H. R. Lloyd	AB	L. Carrol	Sto
K.N. Greatwood	AB	F.H. Meek	Sto
F.E. Fisher	AB	G.W. Sainsbury	Sto
J. Colville	AB	R.E. Taylor	Sto
S. Mercer	Stwd	D.W. Tame	Sto

ACKNOWLEDGEMENTS

The search for *Trooper*'s story took me down some strange submarine avenues, all of which were interesting, though not all were relevant. Several people have been especially helpful, as have a number of institutions. First, grateful thanks to Richard Wraith, whose father was *Trooper*'s Commanding Officer, for writing the Foreword, for Fry's sketches of the boat, for the sketch of his father and for a lot of other help too. Next, my very great thanks go to ex-*Trooper* men Peter Forbes, Allison Gillies and Gordon Ridsdale. This story would have been vastly less complete without their valuable and always generously given time and material. Two other men who had served on her were found but one had only been aboard as a relief for a few weeks during her working-up period and the other was ill. George Malcolmson, Alexandra Havelock and Debbie Corner at the Royal Navy Submarine Museum at Gosport were unfailingly helpful, put up with all my questions and provided access to a wealth of material. George Gardner at Glasgow University Archives introduced me to Scotts Shipbuilding & Engineering Co Ltd's extensive material that even includes the original blueprints for *Trooper*. Roderick Suddaby, Keeper of Documents at the Imperial War Museum, and the IWM photographic archivists helped immensely. Ex-Charioteers Rodney Dove and Dickie Greenwood were able to fill in some blanks about Operation 'Principal' and Pamela Mitchell, whose two books I made much use of, also helped in many ways. The truly awesome amount of material held at the Public Record Office (now National Archives) was the underlying key to all my research. Mr M McAloon of the Ministry of Defence Naval Historical Branch provided helpful information about GA45, as did Herr Thomas Weis of Wuerttembergische Landesbibliothek, Bibliothek fuer Zeitgeschichte in Stuttgart and Herr Wilhelm Knoess of the Maritime Museum in Wilmshaven.

The Internet proved a hugely useful tool and I am particularly indebted to Geoff Chalcraft's site "British Submarines of World War Two" and to "u-boat.net" as well as many others – 143 at the last count! I would also be failing in gratitude not to thank the Submariners Association, from whose web-site I gleaned much useful information and some of whose officials went out of their way to answer questions and try to obtain information for me. Lastly, I must thank Neil Brookes, without whose enquiring mind and practical help I might never have told this story at all.

In telling it, I have come closer to the man I never knew, my half-brother Lt Alick Grant and have developed huge respect for him and all those who served in "The Trade" as the submarine service was and is known. I have also learned an enormous amount about the Second World War as seen through the periscope of a T-class submarine. Apart from the now sadly dwindling number of men who actually went through the experience of that war, none of us can know, and it is quite impossible to imagine, the reality of it. They served with enormous courage and unswerving devotion to duty. Of the all too many who died doing so, we can only salute them, honour them and thank them, because "They gave their tomorrow for our today."

BIBLIOGRAPHY

The list below comprises the main source-books and National Archives documents used. Those marked * were especially useful. Those dealing with particular submarines have the name or names of the boat or boats in Roman type following the reference. In one or two cases where it seemed relevant, the subject matter of a book has been given in italics after the reference.

Akerman, P: *The Encyclopaedia of British Submarines 1901-1955*, **Maritime Books 1989**

Bagnasco, E: *Submarines of World War Two*, **Arms & Armour 1977**

Benyon-Tinker, W E: *Dust Upon the Sea*, **Hodder, 1947** *Levant Schooner Flotilla*

Borghese, J V: *Sea Devils*, **Arrow edition, 1956** Italian 'Maiale' (chariots)

Bryant, B: *Submarine Command*, **Kimber, 1975** Sealion, Safari

*Campbell, N: *Memories of a Young Naval Officer 1936-1947*, **unpub.** Trooper

Chalmers, W S: *Max Horton and the Western Approaches*, **Hodder & Stoughton 1954**

Chapman, P: *Submarine Torbay*, **Hale, 1989** Torbay

Cunningham, A B: *A Sailor's Odyssey*, **Hutchinson, 1951** *C-in-C Mediterranean*

Dickison, A: *Crash Dive!* **Sutton, 1999** Safari

Douglas-Hamilton, Lord J: *The Air Battle for Malta*, **Mainstream, 1981**

Dove, Rodney: *personal communication* **to author, 3rd May 2005**

Evans, A S: *Beneath the Waves – submarine losses 1904-1971*, **Kimber, 1986**

Flack, J: *100 Years of Royal Navy Submarines*, **Airlife, 2002**

*Forbes, Peter: *Record of Events from 5.11.42-15.8.44*, **unpub. Diary** Trooper

Fraser, I: *Frogman VC*, **Angus & Robertson, 1957** X-craft

Fell, W R: *The Sea Our Shield*, **Cassell, 1966** Chariots, X-craft

Gibson, J F: *Dark Seas Above*, **Tempus, 2000** Taurus

Greenland, R T G: *personal communications* **to author**

Hart, S: *Submarine Upholder*, **Oldbourne, 1960** Upholder

    "   : *Discharged Dead*, **White Lion edition, 1976** Truant, Thrasher

Hezlet, A: *HMS Trenchant at War*, Leo Cooper, 2001 Trenchant

"   : *British and Allied Submarine Operations in World War II*, Royal Navy Submarine Museum, 2001

*Hobson, R W: *Chariots of War*, Ulric, 2004 Chariots

Howarth, D: *The Shetland Bus*, Nelson, 1951

Hutchinson, R: *Jane's Submarines*, Ted Smart, 2001

Kemp, Paul: *Underwater Warriors*, Cassell, 1996

*   "   : *The T-Class Submarine*, Naval Institute Press, 1990

"   : *Midget Submarines of the Second World War*, Caxton, 1999

Kemp, P K: *H M Submarines*, Herbert Jenkins, 1952

King, W: *Dive and Attack*, Kimber 1983 Orpheus, Snapper, Trusty, Telemachus

*Lenton, H T: *British Submarines*, Macdonald, 1972

Lipscomb, F W: *The British Submarine*, A & C Black, 1954

Mars, A: *Unbroken*, Muller, 1953 Unbroken

"   : *HMS Thule Intercepts*, Elek, 1956 Thule

"   : *Submarines at War 1939-1945*, Corgi, 1974

Masters, D: *Up Periscope*, Eyre & Spottiswoode 1943

Mitchell, P: *The Tip of the Spear*, Netherwood, 1993 X-craft

*   "   : *Chariots of the Sea*, Netherwood, 1998 Chariots

McGeoch, I: *An Affair of Chances*, Imperial War Museum, 1991 Splendid

Macintyre, D: *Fighting Under the Sea*, Evans, 1965

McLean, R: *Half Seas Under*, Reed, 2001 FF Rubis

Quigley, D J: *Under the Jolly Roger*, Portsmouth Publishing, 1988

Robertson, T: *The Ship With Two Captains*, Evans , 1957 Seraph

Rogers, A: *Churchill's Folly*, Cassell, 2003 *Battle for Leros*

Rohwer, J: *Allied Submarine Attacks of World War Two*, Greenhill Books, 1997

"   : *Axis Submarine Successes of World War Two*, Greenhill Books, 1999

"Seedie": *Seedie's List of Submarine Awards for World War II*, Ripley Registers 1990

*Seligman, A: *War in the Islands*, Sutton, 1997 *Levant Schooner Flotilla*

Shean, M: *Corvette and Submarine*, Shean 1994 edition X-craft

*Simpson, G W G: *Periscope View*, **Macmillan, 1972**

Stevens, J S: *Never Volunteer*, **privately printed, 1971** Thunderbolt, Unruffled

Tall, J J & P Kemp: *H M Submarines in Camera*, **Blitz, 1998**

Thomas, D A: *Submarine Victory*, **Kimber, 1961**

Trenowden, I: *The Hunting Submarine*, **Crecy, 1994 edition** Tally-Ho

Turner, J F: *Periscope Patrol*, **Harrap, 1957**

Underwood, G: *And Some Were Lucky…* , **Linwood, 1996** Otway, Sahib, Tuna

Waldron, J & J Gleason: *The Frogmen*, **Evans Brothers, 1955 edition** Chariots

Warlow, B: *Shore Establishments of the Royal Navy*, **Maritime Books, 2000 edition**

*Warren, C E T & J Benson: *Above Us The Waves*, **Harrap, 1958** Chariots

   "   " : *The Admiralty Regrets…* , **PBC, 1958** Thetis/Thunderbolt

Wingate, J: *The Fighting Tenth*, **Cooper, 1991**

Young, E: *One of Our Submarines*, **Hart-Davies, 1952** Storm

          : *Submarine Memories*, **Gatwick Submarine Archive, nd**

          : *His Majesty's Submarines*, **H M Stationery Office, 1945**

National Archives documents:

ADM 1/13210 Special operations Levant area.

ADM 1/14399 Awards – Trooper

ADM 1/14501 Awards – Trooper

***ADM 1/15764 Report on** *Operation 'Principal'*

ADM 1/18810 Minesweeping in the Meditarranean, 1945.

ADM 1/20027 Naval operations in the Aegean, 7 Oct – 28 Nov 1943.

***ADM 1/20200 Aegean Operations 7 Sep – 28 Nov 1943.**

ADM 1/25845 Memo to Prime Minister re Chariots.

ADM 173 – submarine's logs (all*):

ADM 173/16797 L23

ADM 173/17617 Thunderbolt's **refit.**

ADM 173/17618 Thunderbolt's **log for Nov 1942.**

119

ADM 173/17619 Thunderbolt's log for Dec 1942.

ADM 173/17655 Trooper's log for Aug 1942.

ADM 173/17656 Trooper's log for Sep 1942.

ADM 173/17657 Trooper's log for Oct 1942.

ADM 173/18233 Thunderbolt's log for Jan 1943.

ADM 173/18278 Trooper's log for Apr 1943.

ADM 173/18279 Trooper's log for May 1943.

ADM 173/18280 Trooper's log for Jun 1943

ADM 173/18281 Trooper's log for Jul 1943.

ADM 173/19694 Spearhead's log for July 1945

(*Op. 'Sabre'* – CO Lt Cdr R E Youngman).

ADM 199 – submarine's patrol reports:

ADM 199/285 Seal, Orzel, Taku, **etc.**

ADM 199/286 Tribune, Trident, **etc.**

ADM 199/288 H34, H49, L23, Salmon **(Lt O F Lancaster), etc.**

ADM 199/418 War Diaries, Aberdeen, Blyth and Dundee.

ADM 199/535 Special Operations by ships, LCT's etc.

ADM 199/648 War Diaries: Mediterranean 1942, etc.

ADM 199/1115 Various submarines reports.

ADM 199/1205 Includes *Lt R P Webb***'s time in USA with P555.**

ADM 199/1830 L23

***ADM 199/1833 Sailing orders for** Trooper **and P311; also P311's passage report.**

ADM 199/1843 Saracen.

***ADM 199/1846 Sailing orders for** Thunderbolt.

ADM 199/1849 Traveller.

ADM 199/1876 Spearhead **and** Spark.

ADM 199/1881 Saracen's pr's and Lt Clarabut as senior officer at Haifa.

***ADM 199/1923 Includes Op. 'Principal' and Aegean operations, inc.** Trooper's **loss.**

ADM 199/1925 War History including Thunderbolt, P311, Trooper, **etc.**

<u>Others:</u>

*ADM 223/579 Lead up and background to *Operation 'Principal'*

ADM 267/114 War damage to submarines. Includes photographs of HMS *Medway* sinking.

AIR 2/8438 Proposals for and development of schemes to transport chariots by air.

*DEFE 2/842 *Folbots.*

DEFE 2/901 Uffa Fox Pontoon.

HS 5/585 SOE in Greece.

HS 5/714 SOE in Greece, including Operation 'Archive'

INDEX

"We Dive at Dawn", 89
6 Commando, 89
12 Commando, 89
269 Squadron RAF, 21

A

Accacio, 105
Adam, P.M., 114
Aegean, 1, 6, 11, 101, 111, 119, 120
Alexander, A.V., First Lord, 26
Alexandria, 25, 41, 80, 94
Algiers, 11, 72, 79, 80, 82, 83, 85, 86, 87
Amorgos, 105
Anderson, A.W., 114
Antikythira, *103*
Anti-Paxos, 69, 70
Ardanaddam, 24
Area QBB.65, 87
Argostoli (Cephalonia), 69, 71
Arran, 23
Artful, HMS, 19
Arthur, HMS, 8, 27, 29
August Leonhardt, 23
Avonvale, HMS, 34
Axis forces, 66, 103

B

Baalbek, 92
Balkwill, First Lt Robert, 85
Bari, 90, 91
Barry, Rear Admiral Claud, 84
Bastia, 20, 86
Beaufighters, 87
Beckinsale, Capt S., *105*
Beirut, 11, 39, 87, 91, 92, 94, 100, 101,
    102, 105, 107, 108
Bengough, I.D., 114
Berey, PO, 68
Bergius, Sub-Lt Adam, DSC, 86
Bishop Rock, 34, 35
Blyth, HMS, 23, 34, 120

Bocca Grande, 78
Bombay, 104
Borghese, Commander Prince Valerio,
    27
Briggs, Sub-Lt K.M., DSC, 86
Brindisi-Durazzo route, 98
British United Press, 80
Britton, Gus, 80
Bromage, Lt T.H., 86
Brotherston, A., 114
Browne, Commander H.C., 86
Bulgaria, 107
Bute Sound, 23
Buxton, Chief Petty Officer, 47
Buxton, Chief ERA Stanley, 68

C

Cachalot, 108
Cagliari, 41, 42, 47
Calolino, 112
Cammel Laird, Birkenhead, 47
Campbell, Sub-Lt The Hon Neil, RN,
    14, 68, 76, 83, 84, 102, 110 111, 117
Canada, 23
Cant Z506, 99
Cape Bonifati, 76
Cape Cabonara, 79
Cape Dukato, 69, 97, 98
Cape Milazzo, 48, 73, 74
Cape Peloro, 74
Cape Polinuro, 77
Cape Rasocolmo, 74
Cape St Vito, 72
Cape Vaticano, 73
Capo San Vito, 77
Capo Sta Maria, 99
Capri, 78, 85
Caproni 311, 78
Carling, T.M., 114
Carrol, L., 114
Carter, Leading Seaman, 44
Cavtal, 99

Cayley, Lt Cdr R.D., 38, 39, 40, 41, 42, 49, 67
Cedars of Lebanon, 92
Cephalonia, 11, 68
Chariots, 10, 11, 28, 35, 47, 50, 51, 65, 68, 117, 118, 119
Charnock, F., 114
Chatham Dockyard, 28
Chios, 103
Chiver, R.S., 114
Churchill, Sir Winston, 6, 25
Ciclone, 65
Cicogna, 77
Clarabut, Lt G.S.C., DSO, RN, 11, 19, 95, 96, 97, 98, 100, 101, 108, 111, 120
Cloch Point, 19
Clyde, 10, 17, 18, 20, 29, 89
Colville, J., 114
Colvin, Lt Cdr G.R., 84
Constantinos, 105
Cook, Lt, 44, 65
Coombe, Lt J.W., 67
Cope, H.C., 114
Corfu, 11, 68, 70
Cornelius, J., 114
Courtney, Maj. R.J.C., MC, 88
Crawford, Lt M.L., 85
Crete, 91, 103
Crossland, F., 114
Crouch, Lt Cdr Cecil, 40, 77, 84
Cunningham, Admiral Sir Andrew B., 49, 66, 82, 83, 111
Cunningham, Sir John H.D., 111
Curry, T., 114
Cutty Sark, HMS, 34
Cyclades, 103, 105
Cyprus, 103

D

Damascus, 93
Daniell, Lt A.R., 48
Davies, G., 114
Davis Submarine Escape Apparatus [DSEA]., 26
Devonport, 35, 41

Dewhurst, Lt Cdr R.H., 89
Dodecanese, 11, 103, 104, 105, 112
Dolphin, HMS, 26
Doro Channel, 101, 102
Dove, Sub-Lt Rodney G., 29, 30, 44, 51, 66, 115, 117
Drache, 107
Drummond, Lt St Clair Ford, 39
Dymoke-Byrne, Lt J.J., RNR, 86

E

Edrachillis Bay., 34
Eggesworth, HMS, 87
Eighth Army, 67, 68
Eleni S, 112
Euterpe, Italian corvette, 20, 86

F

Faber, Lt M.E. 67
Far East, 24, 100, 105
Farnell, J.B., 114
Fawkes, 77, 85
Fawkes, Capt. G.B.H., 66
Fell, Commander W.R. 'Tiny', 25, 26, 28, 29, 38, 117
Fenn, W.C.E., DSM., 108, 114
Ferrier, 46, 52, 65, 66
First Submarine Flotilla, 37, 70, 71, 92, 104, 107
Fisher, F.E., 114
Fleming, S., 114
Folbot Company, 88
Forbes, Peter, 14, 31, 36, 38, 39, 42, 45, 49, 68, 69, 71, 72, 73, 74, 79, 80, 82, 84, 86, 89, 90, 91, 92, 93, 95, 96, 98, 100, 101, 115
Forth, HMS, 20, 21, 22, 23, 24, 82
France, 35
Freel, L/S, 44, 51, 52
Fry, E.A.W.V., DSM, 101, 108, 114
Funchal, 41
Furnell, E.C., 114

123

G

GA45, 112, 113, 115
Gambut, 103
Gamma, 65
Gateshead, 24
Germany, 103
Gibraltar, 29, 34, 37
Gilbert, J.B., 114
Gillies, Alison, 19, 21, 24, 115
Gillies, Nessie, 21, 22
Giraud, General, 86
Gozo, 87
Granito, 20
Grant, Lt L.A.S., DSC, RN, 5, 6, 19, 101, 108, 109, 110, 114, 116
Graph, HMS, 21, 23
Greatwood, K.N., 114
Greenberg, Julian, journalist, 80
Greenland, Lt 'Dickie', RNVR, 35, 46, 52, 65, 66, 117
Greenock, 17, 18, 20, 23
Griechenland Aegaeis, 112
Grogan, Sub-Lt Jack, 38
Guelma, SS, 41
Gulf of Taranto, 39, 40, 99

H

Haifa, 111, 120
Halifax, 41
Harwood, Admiral Sir Henry, 111
Hastings, Gen. Sir Ismay, 25
Hedgehog, HMS, 105, 106
Hermes, HMS, 85
Hind, G.W., 114
HMDY Chatham, 38, 105
Holy Loch, 20, 21, 22, 23, 24, 25, 31, 32, 35
Horsea, 26
Horton, H.G., 114
Horton, Vice-Admiral Sir Max, 25
Hudson aircraft, 21
Hunt, Lt George, 85
Hutchison, J.N., Shipyard Director, 17

I

Iceland, 21
Imperial War Museum, 14, 115, 118
Inchmarnock, 20, 22, 23
Ionides, Capt H.M.C., 89, 102
Iscolelli Point, 73
Isle of Lewis, 26
Isola di Ustica, 43
Italy, 69, 72, 90

J

J.1108, 17, 18
James Watt Dock, 23
Jervis, HMS, 25, 112
Jewell, Lt 'Bill' , 86
John Brown's yard, 82

K

Kalimnos, 104, 112
Kames Bay, 22
Karpathos, 103
Kaso Straits, 105
Kasos, 103, 107
Kephallonia, 103
Kerr, 48
Klepper, Johann, German tailor, 88
Kos, 102, 103, 104, 105, 112
Kythira, 103

L

L23, 28, 34, 119, 120
La Capricieuse, 35
La Cordilière, 23
La Maddalena, 11, 42, 47
Lancaster, Lt O.F., DSC, 21, 109, 114
Land's End, 36
Larisa, 103
Larkin, Lt, 68
Lawson, C.C., 114
Lazaretto Creek, 34, 39
Leatham, Vice-Admiral Sir Ralph, 49, 111

124

Legg, A.F., 114
Leros, 11, 102, 103, 104, 105, 106, 107, 111, 118
Lesbos, 103
Levant Schooner Flotilla, 105, 117, 118
Levant Schooner LS.8, 106
Levkas, 68, 97
Libra, 77
Libya, 103
Limnos, 103
Linosa, 41
Linton, Cdr, 84
Lloyd, H.R., 114
Loch Cairnbawn, 10, 26, 29, 31, 34, 93
Loch Erisort, 26, 34
Loch Long, 19, 21
Loch Ranza, 23
Lofoten Islands, Norway, 23
Luftwaffe, 39, 103

M

Mackenzie, Lt Cdr A.J., 67
Maddalena, 48
Maiale, 25, 27
Maidstone, HMS, 66, 80, 82, 83, 85
Malta, 10, 11, 29, 30, 31, 34, 35, 36, 37, 38, 39, 41, 42, 48, 49, 66, 67, 68, 69, 71, 72, 82, 83, 86, 87, 90, 91, 92, 106, 111, 117
Marcello Class, 101
Marguerite, 107
Marittimo Island, 38, 41, 72
Mather, J., 114
Mathias, Mrs, 18
McGeoch, Lt Ian, 85, 118
Mediterranean, 1, 6, 23, 29, 30, 38, 41, 43, 48, 49, 66, 68, 80, 83, 84, 87, 97, 103, 105, 108, 111, 112, 117, 120
Medusa, HMS, 87
Medway, HMS, 37, 66, 70, 92, 94, 95, 111, 121
Medway II, HMS, 37, 66, 70, 92
Meek, F.H., 114
Mekong river, 86
Mercer, S., 114

Messina, 11, 71, 73, 76
Micca Class, 100
Middle East, *103*
Miers, Lt Cdr Toby, VC, *105*
Milazzo, 11, 76
Mills, R.W., 114
Miln, 46, 65
Minerva, HMS, 20, 86
Mitchell, Pamela, 35, 115
Molmat, 99
Mott, Stoker A.H., 108, 114
Müller, Generalleutnant, 104
Mull of Kintyre, 34
Murmansk, 26

N

Naples, 11, 48, 71, 73, 78
Neist Point, 34
Nelson, HMS, 86, 118
Norway, 20, 23, 26, 27
Operation 'Anklet', 23
Operation 'Eisbär', 104
Operation 'Entertain', 89
Operation 'Husky', 68
Operation 'Principal', 11, 40, 47, 66, 67, 115, 119, 121
Operation 'Sabre', 86
Operation 'Title', 36
Operation 'Torch', 67
Outer Hebrides, 26

P

P222, 67
P311, 10, 11, 25, 28, 30, 33, 34, 35, 38, 39, 41, 42, 43, 47, 48, 49, 67, 120
P37, 47
P43, 47, 48
P46, 46, 47, 48
P48, 67
P63, 20
P66, 23
P213, 20
P614, 89
P615, 89

Palermo Bay, 42
Palmer, Derek, 49
Pantellaria, 37, 38, 42, 72, 87
Penn, HMS, 112
Periscope View, 67, 119
Perisher exercise, 23
Peters, M, 114
Phillips, Capt G.C., 67
Pietro Micca, 11, 100, 101, 108
Port Argostoli, 68
Port Said, 11, 93, 94, 95, 96
Portsmouth, 35, 118
Preveza, 71
Prinz Eugen, 26
Promontorio del Gargano, 90
Proteus, 23

Q

Queen Elizabeth, HMS, 25

R

RAF Wellington, 84
Rayner, Sub-Lt W.A.T., RNR, 95
Regent, HMS, 86
Regia Aeronautica, 39
Rhodes, 11, 101, 103, 104
Ribbans, S.E., 114
Ridsdale, Gordon, 94, 115
Robinson, Ldg Stoker R.N. DSM, 101, 108, 114
Rodney, HMS, 29, 30, 51, 86, 115, 117
Rohwer, Jürgen, *107*
Rommel's Army, 80
Ronaldsay, 80
Rorqual, HMS, 89, 104, 111
Rothesay Bay, 23, 26
Royal Air Force, 84, 103
Royal Glasgow Institute of Fine Arts, 18
Royal Navy, 1, 6, 8, 10, 18, 35, 41, 85, 115, 117, 118, 119
Royal Navy Submarine Museum, 14
Royal Oak, HMS, 6
Royal Scottish Academy, 18

Royal Scottish Society of Painters in Watercolours, 18
Royalist, HMS, 23
Ruck-Keene, Capt Phillip, 66, 71, 91, 92, 94, 102
Ruston, Ldg Seaman, DSM, 101, 108, 114
Ryder, J.S., 114

S

S. Catello, 91
S24, renamed *P555*, 68
Sagona, 25
Sahib, HMS, 85, 86, 119
Sainsbury, G.W., 114
Salmon, HMS, 109, 120
Salonika, *11, 102, 103*
Samos, *102, 103, 104*
Samothraki, *103*
Saracen, HMS, 20, 28, 29, 34, 86, 120
Sardinia, 42, 46, 79
Scirè, 27
Scotland, 21, 26, 27, 31
Scotts Shipbuilding & Engineering Co Ltd, Greenock, 14, 17, 115
Sealion, HMS, 23
Seraph, HMS, 86, 111, 118
Severn, HMS, 104
Shean, Lt Max, DSO, 86
Shetlands, 20
Shiant Isles, 34
Sicily, 1, 20, 38, 42, 68, 72, 74, 86, 97, 99, 105
Simpson, Capt G.W.G. 'Shrimp', 29, 37, 39, 40, 41, 43, 46, 48, 65, 66, 67, 119
Skiathos Channel, 102
Skinner, H., 114
Sladen suits, 44
Sladen, Cdr Geoffrey, 26, 29, 38
Sleep, PO, DSM, 108
Sleep, R.B., DSM, 114
Smethurst, F., 114
South African Naval Forces, 38
Spark, HMS, 19, 120
Spearhead, HMS, 85, 120

126

Spitfires, *104*
Splendid, HMS, 85, 86, 118
Sporades, 103
St Clair Ford, Lt, D, 67
St John, Lt Michael, 39, 111
Stanley, Lt E.S. 47
Stevens, Sub-Lt H.L., 68
Stevens, J.S., Lt DSO DSC RN, 46
Stillwell, C.J., 114
Stobbie, J., 114
Straits of Otranto, 89, 99
Stromboli, 76
Strombolioccio, 76
Strongbow, HMS, 19
Sumner, H.G., 114
Sutherland, 26
Sweden, 27
Swordfish, HMS, 40, 87

T

Tactician, HMS, 100
Talbot, HMS, 66, 87
Tame, D.W., 114
Tarantini, 41
Taranto, 66
Taylor, R.E., 114
T-class submarines, 14, 18, 46, 108
Tenth Submarine Flotilla, 66
Thasos, *103*
The National Archives (Public Record Office), 14
The Star, newspaper, 80
Thetis, HMS, 25, 40, 47, 119
Thompson, L., 114
Thompson, Sqn Ldr, 21
Thunderbolt, HMS, 11, 25, 24, 28, 30, 31, 34, 35, 36, 39, 40, 41, 42, 43, 44, 46, 47, 48, 49, 50, 52, 65, 67, 77, 84, 119, 120
Tigris, HMS, 83
Tirpitz, HMS, 27, 36
Titania, HMS, 26, 27, 32, 33, 34, 35
Torbay, HMS, 105, 106, 112, 117
Traveller, HMS, 18, 39, 66, 67, 120
Trespasser, HMS, 24

Tribune, HMS, 19, 38, 80, 120
Trident, HMS, 26, 120
Tripoli, 67, 68
Tripp, F.W., 114
Triton, HMS, 14
Trondhjemsfjord, 27
Troon, 23
Troop Transport Aircraft, 38
Trooper, HMS, 1, 5, 6, 8, 10, 14, 16, 17, 18, 19, 20, 21, 22, 24, 25, 28, 29, 30, 31,33, 34, 35, 36, 37, 38, 39, 40, 41, 42, 43, 44, 45, 47, 48, 49, 50, 51, 52, 65, 67, 68, 70, 71, 72, 73, 74, 75, 76, 77, 78, 79, 80, 84, 85, 86, 87, 89, 90, 91, 92, 93, 94, 95, 97, 98, 99, 100, 101, 102, 103, 105, 106, 107, 108, 110, 111, 112, 115, 117, 119, 120
Turbulent, HMS, 84
Turkey, 89
Tyrrhenian Sea, 11, 20, 37, 72, 76

U

U-335, 20
U-570, 21
U-644, 22
Uffa Fox Pontoon, 88, 121
UJ2145, 112
Ulpio Traiano, 65
Ultor, HMS, 85
Una, HMS, 38
Unbending, HMS, 47
Unison, HMS, 47, 87
United Kingdom, 30
Unrivalled, HMS, 105
Unruffled, HMS, 46, 85, 92, 119
Unruly, HMS, 105
Unseen, HMS, 85
Upright, HMS, 40, 47, 108
Ursula, HMS, 88
Ustica, 11, 43, 48, 50, 84
Utmost, HMS, 67

V

Valiant, HMS, 25

Vaternish Point, 34
Vickers Armstrong, 23, 28
Vieste, 90
Viminale, SS, 51, 52, 65

W

Walker, D., 114
Watson, A/CPO, DSM, *108*
Watson, J.A., DSM, 114
Webb, Lt R.P., RN, 68, 69, 70, 71
Whatley, E., 114
Whiting, J.B., 114
Williams, L., 114
World War II, 6, 8, 12, 118
Worthy, AB., 44, 65
Wraith, Lt J.S., DSO, DSC, RN, 17, 18, 20, 40, 42, 45, 47, 68, 72, 73, 74, 75, 78, 79, 80, 84, 89, 90, 91, 94, 95, 101, 106, 108
Wraith, Richard, 1, 7, 115

X

XE-4, midget submarine, 86

Y

Yarrow's of Scotstoun, 85
Yeoman, R.A., 114
Youngman, Lt R.E., RNR, 85, 86, 108, 120

Z

Zante, 69, 89, 97